COME HOME

A CALL BACK TO FAITH

JAMES MACDONALD

LifeWay Press®
Nashville, Tennessee

Published by LifeWay Press®
© 2014 James MacDonald

ISBN 9781430035183
Item 005682240

Dewey decimal classification: 234.4
Subject headings: REGENERATION (CHRISTIANITY) \ CHRISTIAN LIFE \ REPENTANCE

To order additional copies of this resource, write to LifeWay Church Resources Customer Service; One LifeWay Plaza; Nashville, TN 37234-0113; fax 615.251.5933; phone toll free 800.458.2772; order online at *www.lifeway.com;* email *orderentry@lifeway.com;* or visit the LifeWay Christian Store serving you.

Printed in the United States of America

Adult Ministry Publishing
LifeWay Church Resources
One LifeWay Plaza
Nashville, TN 37234-0152

CONTENTS

THE AUTHOR

JAMES MACDONALD has committed his life to the unapologetic proclamation of God's Word. He is the founder and senior pastor of Harvest Bible Chapel, one of the fastest-growing churches in the Chicago area, reaching more than 13,000 lives each weekend. Heard on the "Walk in the Word" radio and television broadcasts, his practical teaching is also accessed by thousands online. Through James's leadership and by God's grace, Harvest Bible Fellowship, the church-planting ministry he founded in 2002,has planted more than one hundred churches across North America and around the world.

Born in London, Ontario, Canada, James received his master's degree from Trinity Evangelical Divinity School in Deerfield, Illinois, and his doctorate from Phoenix Seminary. He and his wife, Kathy, have three adult children and reside in Chicago. For more information about James and these ministries, visit *www.harvestbible.org* or *www.walkintheword.org*.

Other books and Bible studies by James MacDonald:

Always True: God's Promises When Life Is Hard Bible study (LifeWay, 2011)

Always True: God's Five Promises for When Life Is Hard (Moody, 2011)

Authentic: Developing the Disciplines of a Sincere Faith Bible study (LifeWay, 2013)

Authentic (Moody, 2013)

Come Home (Moody, 2013)

Downpour: He Will Come to Us like the Rain Bible study (LifeWay, 2006)

Downpour: He Will Come to Us like the Rain (B&H, 2006)

God Wrote a Book (Crossway, 2002)

Gripped by the Greatness of God Bible study (LifeWay, 2005)

Gripped by the Greatness of God (Moody, 2005)

Have the Funeral small-group study (LifeWay, 2011)

I Really Want to Change … So, Help Me God (Moody, 2000)

Lord, Change Me (Moody, 2012)

Lord, Change My Attitude Bible study (LifeWay, 2008)

Lord, Change My Attitude … Before It's Too Late (Moody, 2001)

Seven Words to Change Your Family (Moody, 2001)

10 Choices: A Proven Plan to Change Your Life Forever (Thomas Nelson, 2008)

When Life Is Hard Bible study (LifeWay, 2010)

When Life Is Hard (Moody, 2010)

Vertical Church Bible study (LifeWay, 2012)

Vertical Church (David C Cook, 2012)

Visit *www.lifeway.com/jamesmacdonald* for information about James MacDonald resources published by LifeWay.

INTRODUCTION

What do you think of when you hear the word *wanderer?* Somebody who's lost their way, who's going through life with no sense of direction or purpose? Somebody who's pulled in one direction and then another without a solid value system to guide them?

What about this: someone who embraced the truth of the gospel but then turned their back on God and went their own way? Can you imagine such a tragic decision? For some reason they used to love God and attend church, but now they've wandered away. I've known the pain of seeing a loved one wander from God, and perhaps you have too.

A short passage in the Book of James describes that situation and admonishes us to go get the wanderers and bring them home. Based on that passage, this Bible study will develop in you a greater heart for the hurting people who've wandered away from God and will identify from Scripture a number of actions you can take to bring them home.

Wanderers come in both genders, in many ages, and with unique struggles. Yet they fall into several categories as defined on the pages of Scripture. We'll study Peter, Thomas, Samson, and the prodigal son and let them represent particular types of wanderers God loves and wants to bring home. I hope you'll learn to recognize the wanderers you encounter, love them the way God does, and follow His leading to bring them back.

God has an urgent message for wanderers: come home! And He has an urgent message for you: go get them! As you complete this study, let God fill you with His love for the wanderers you know. Then be obedient to go get them and bring them back home to the waiting arms of their Father.

HOW TO GET THE MOST FROM THIS STUDY

1. Attend each group experience.
   - Watch the DVD teaching.
   - Participate in the group discussions.
2. Complete the content in this Bible study book.
   - Read the daily lessons and complete the learning activities.
   - Memorize each week's suggested memory verse.
   - Ask God to show you how to bring home the wanderers you know, as well as ways you've wandered from His truth.
   - Go deeper by reading James MacDonald's book *Come Home* (Moody Publishers, 2013; ISBN 978-0-8024-5718-9).

WEEK 1

GO GET THE WANDERER

START

WELCOME TO THIS GROUP DISCUSSION OF *COME HOME*.

To facilitate introductions and to focus on the theme of *Come Home,* spend a few minutes talking as a group about what it feels like to be physically lost. Use the following questions as the basis of your discussion.

- When have you been physically lost as a child or as an adult? What did being lost feel like?

- What dangers threaten a person who's physically lost?

- How did you find your way back home or to your destination?

This study is about Christians who wander away from God. What ideas or images come to mind when you hear the word *wanderer?*

What does it look like to wander from God? Why is that dangerous?

To prepare for the DVD segment, read aloud the following verses.

> *My brothers, if anyone among you wanders from the truth and someone brings him back, let him know that whoever brings back a sinner from his wandering will save his soul from death and will cover a multitude of sins.*
> **JAMES 5:19-20**

WATCH

COMPLETE THE VIEWER GUIDE BELOW AS YOU WATCH DVD SESSION 1.

The _____ exists.

No one is beyond the reach of God's _____.

To wander: to proceed without a proper sense of _____

Both things happen: people just foolishly wander off, or relationships come and get in someone's head and _____ them away.

Wandering begins with an initial _____.

People who have wandered from the truth are not in the light; they're in _____.

The _____ is possible.

Almighty God _____ back wanderers. He restores them. He forgives them. He celebrates them.

Probably the person _____ to you, God's going to have to touch someone else's heart to go get them.

There are people right now who are out there _____.
Who do you need to go find?

The _____ are high.

False professions and fake Christians leave and never come back. _____ Christians, though they may wander, come back.

The _____ is great.

The past can be forgiven. The hurts can be healed. The sin can be atoned for. That's the great message of the _____.

DISCUSS THE DVD SEGMENT WITH YOUR GROUP, USING THE QUESTIONS BELOW.

What did you like best in James's teaching? Why?

What emotions are you experiencing after hearing James teach about people who wander away from God and about the importance of bringing them back?

What are some distractions or influences that might lead Christians to wander away from the truth?

What is God's attitude toward Christians who've wandered from Him?

Discuss James's statement: "False professions and fake Christians leave and never come back. True Christians, though they may wander, come back."

What risks are involved in trying to bring a wanderer back to God?

In what ways have you wandered from God? What brought you back home, and how did you experience restoration?

Application. This week be aware of anyone you encounter in your normal routine who's wandering from God. Note signs that indicate they're wandering. Also look for any signs that they want to come home. Ask God to show you ways you could help bring them back. During the next group session, be prepared to talk about anything the Lord shows you.

This week's Scripture memory.

> *There will be more joy in heaven over one sinner who repents than over ninety-nine righteous persons who need no repentance.*
> **LUKE 15:7**

Assignment. Read week 1 and complete the activities before the next group experience. Consider going deeper into this content by reading chapter 1 in James MacDonald's book *Come Home* (Moody Publishers, 2013).

GO GET THE WANDERER

In 1961 Dion, one of those single-name artists, recorded a song called "The Wanderer." If you know the song, you're probably singing it right now in your head. It reached number 2 on the charts and is now listed in *Rolling Stone* magazine's list of the five hundred greatest songs of all time.

In many ways that song captures the adventure, danger, and futility in a wanderer's life. His life roams around and never settles down. His relationships are temporary. He doesn't really connect with where he is, where he's been, or where he's going. He's lost, vaguely wondering whether there's something better but caught in the not-so-merry-go-round of restless searching. It's hard for a wanderer even to admit that he's not getting anywhere in all this wandering. But when it comes to wandering from God, a life of aimlessness can have eternal consequences.

The title of this week's study expresses a command: go get the wanderer. Our focal passage is a sober call to action found at the conclusion of the Book of James. It drives home the importance of bringing a wanderer out of his clueless searching and into a life of purposeful spiritual direction. The message is clear: go get the wanderer!

DAY 1

SOME CHRISTIANS WANDER

Have you ever had the experience of God's Word reaching your heart and rocking you to the core? That happened to me when I was reading the Book of James and these words grabbed my heart:

> *My brothers, if anyone among you wanders from the truth and someone brings him back, let him know that whoever brings back a sinner from his wandering will save his soul from death and will cover a multitude of sins.*
> **JAMES 5:19-20**

What do you find new or interesting about this passage? What questions does it raise?

This passage is the foundation of this Bible study. We'll let it speak to us about family members and friends who've wandered from the truth and need to come home to God.

THE PROBLEM

Men and women everywhere have a tendency to wander—even in the church. That's why James addressed the problem in his practical letter to believers. He ended his letter with a call to go get people who'd lost their way.

The expression **"My brothers" (v. 19)** aims to get our attention: "Now don't miss this last thing!" James's real concern wasn't wandering people in general but wandering Christians. He was calling on brothers to care for brothers. He wanted sisters to look out for sisters. He was thinking about people who embraced the truth of the gospel of Jesus Christ and then wandered away from their former commitment.

Who in your life fits the description of a wanderer—a Christian who's wandered away from God?

Why do you think that person has wandered away from the Lord?

James was emphatic: "My brothers and sisters—family of God! Go get the wanderer!" Wandering was a problem then, and it is now. Going astray is a reality we have to deal with if we're really family, if we're truly brothers and sisters in Christ.

Notice James's next phrase: **"My brothers, if anyone among you …"** (v. 19). He was talking about people among us, folks who were once with us. These are fellow Christians you could probably think of right now—people who used to sit behind you in church or were part of your Bible study class. James was saying it's very important that you find out what happened to them. He was saying, "Listen up! Go get the wanderers!"

WHAT IT MEANS TO WANDER

James continued, **"My brothers, if anyone among you wanders …"** (v. 19). The New American Standard Bible says "strays." The Greek term is *planetai,* from which we get our word *planet*. In New Testament times, people obviously didn't have Google Maps™ or a GPS. Ancient people kept track of direction when they traveled by using the sun and stars. Early on, they used the planets as guides. Unfortunately, the planets changed locations in the sky, so the results weren't completely reliable. The idea that the planets shifted—*planetai*—came to designate anything that moved or wandered.

Here's a good definition of wandering: *to proceed without a proper sense of direction.* That's what wandering is—spinning out of orbit.

Has that definition ever described your life? In what way?

James went on to say:

> *My brothers, if anyone among you wanders from the truth*
> *and someone brings him back …*
> **JAMES 5:19**

From what do people wander? Verse 19 identifies that: the truth. This term doesn't invite creative translation; it's straightforward. The center of our lives—the core—is what we believe. God has made some declarations of truth, and we believe them and build our lives on them. When we wander, we wander from the truth. And we wander into error.

The verse doesn't say "wanders from Jesus," but of course, Jesus *is* Truth. He said, "I am … the truth" (John 14:6). So in that sense we could say a person wanders from Jesus. It doesn't say "wanders from the church," although the church is implied in the context since James was writing to a body of believers. So this passage implies that when people wander from the truth that once formed the basis of their belief system, they wander from the Lord and the church.

When wanderers come back, they come back to a place and to a people, and certainly they come back to a Person—God. They also come back to the truth itself. Jesus said in John 17:17, "Sanctify them in the truth; your word is truth." This is very good news because it's a frightening thing to live life apart from the truth of God's Word.

How does God's Word keep a believer grounded in the truth?

Notice the text says, **"If … someone brings him back …" (Jas. 5:19).** Someone has to go get the wanderers. God will reach them through a person. Maybe that person is you.

We're all familiar with various methods for reaching people for Christ. But most of the time, authentic life change in people happens face-to-face and life on life. That's especially true in bringing a wanderer back to God. Don't sail a gospel blimp over their neighborhood or hope they drive by a billboard. You won't be able to simply put a doorknocker invitation on the wanderer's house and then wait to see them at church. It's going to take direct contact and a personal touch.

God's Word says **"someone brings him back" (v. 19).** Someone goes and brings the wanderer back. Don't avoid the tension of a personal contact. Go get the wanderer.

Begin to ask yourself, *Who is it for me? Whom do I need to go find? Who's not following the Lord right now whom I love and care for?* They may not know anyone else who can share the hope you have to offer.

Think about one or more wanderers you know. Begin to ask God regularly how He wants you to bring these wanderers home.

When we start caring about wanderers the way God does, we can expect a certain weight of sorrow in the effort. But the joy He promises will make it worthwhile. Go get the wanderer.

DAY 2

GOD OFFERS A REMEDY

The Bible frequently compares people to sheep, animals that are known for wandering away from the fold. Isaiah wrote this:

> *All we like sheep have gone astray;*
> *We have turned—every one—to his own way.*
> **ISAIAH 53:6**

How do people go astray and follow their own way?

Isaiah was talking about our natural tendency to choose our own path in life instead of following God's way. We see it in many people in the Bible, and we see it in our own lives. It's the way we're wired as fallen human beings. So when we talk about wandering from the truth, that's something that comes very naturally to us.

Yesterday we started looking at a passage from the Book of James that emphasizes the importance of identifying wanderers and bringing them back to God:

> *My brothers, if anyone among you wanders from the truth*
> *and someone brings him back, let him know that whoever*
> *brings back a sinner from his wandering will save his soul*
> *from death and will cover a multitude of sins.*
> **JAMES 5:19-20**

There are two possible ways to understand the word *wanders*. One kind of wandering has a person in mind who just wandered off: "Whoa! I'm over here now. I didn't have any plan. I didn't expect to end up in this place. I just woke up one day and wasn't where I used to be."

But another kind of wandering describes a person who was drawn away, a person who was taken by a wolf. Jesus talked about wolves in sheep's clothing:

*Beware of false prophets, who come to you in sheep's clothing
but inwardly are ravenous wolves.*
MATTHEW 7:15

These lost sheep used to believe the truth, but now they believe error. They used to listen to what was right, but they started listening to what was wrong, and it drew them away. Someone came and got them and took them away from the truth.

How can believers today be drawn away from following Jesus?

Both things happen: people foolishly wander off, or negative, destructive relationships come along, get in someone's head, and draw them away. So we have two wanderers in mind: the foolish "How did I get over here?" wanderer and the person who's been led away by someone. Both are forms of wandering that James challenges us to address.

It's easy for people to wander away from God. Even believers can drift when they become distracted or aren't intentional about their spiritual growth and obedience to Christ. But no matter how they turn away, God loves wanderers, and He wants us to bring them home.

GOD'S HEART FOR THE WANDERER
In Luke 15 Jesus revealed God's heart for the wanderer:

*What man of you, having a hundred sheep, if he has lost one
of them, does not leave the ninety-nine in the open country,
and go after the one that is lost, until he finds it?*
LUKE 15:4

What do the sheep represent?

What do Jesus' words mean for the wanderer?

Now here's some really good news for wanderers: God receives them back. He welcomes them. He restores them. He forgives them. He even *celebrates* them! Jesus said:

> *There will be more joy in heaven over one sinner who repents than over ninety-nine righteous persons who need no repentance.*
> **LUKE 15:7**

What do the two previous verses show about God's heart?

Heaven is fired up every time a wanderer returns. God's desire is for wanderers to come home—and for you to go bring them back.

Wanderers need us to find them. That's what this study is all about. We're praying for the same heart Jesus expressed as He looked at the crowds following Him:

> *When he saw the crowds, he had compassion for them, because they were harassed and helpless, like sheep without a shepherd.*
> **MATTHEW 9:36**

Jesus left heaven to come find us when we were wandering. If someone you know has wandered from the truth, do you have any compassion for this person? Is your heart heavy for them, for the hard situations in which they find themselves? God loves the wanderer the *same* as He loves you and me, and He wants us to go get them.

If you've identified someone who's wandering, imagine what it's like for him to be in darkness with no sense of direction. Spend time today praying for that person: "I don't know what he was doing last night. I don't know where he's going this weekend. But he's lost in the darkness. Meet him there, Lord, and guide him back to Your truth."

SEEKING THE WANDERER

When you think of someone who's wandered from the Lord—a son, a daughter, a sister, or a brother—it's the people we love most, the people closest to us. Those are the people to whom our hearts immediately go out. But let me make a painful observation: sometimes the obvious wanderer isn't the person you'll be able to go get.

Why might it be difficult to bring back the wanderer who's closest to you?

Chances are you've probably already tried to reach out to a wanderer who's closest to you. Reading this might motivate you to confront them: "It's time, man! You're coming back right now!" That's not going to go well because you've probably had this conversation before. Your wanderer's guard is up, and sometimes a family member is the last person the wanderer will listen to.

God's going to have to touch someone else's heart to go get them. They're probably going to have to hear it from another person. So diligently pray for the obvious wanderer, but go get the less obvious one God puts on your heart. Then trust God to put the one closest to you on someone else's heart. I'm not saying you shouldn't do anything, but realize that you may not be the point person God will use in your loved one's life.

Instead, go get the less obvious wanderer God puts on your heart—someone you knew in school or haven't talked to for a long time who'd be surprised to hear your voice. You might have to make an effort to find him or her. Maybe it's a friend you've grown apart from or someone you used to see in church.

A woman in our church wrote a beautiful letter to a couple she used to sit near every week. They used to talk, and she knew their first names. They'd pray together before or after the service. Suddenly she didn't see them. They were just gone. A few months later she saw the wife in a grocery store. She asked, "What happened to you? Are you OK?" The wife had to hurry, but it was obvious she was really burdened. Something had happened; maybe she was wounded. So our member wrote her a letter. She's trying to get those wanderers. Let God touch your heart with a person like that.

> **Does such a person come to mind? Think of someone you used to see at church, at the gym, or at school or work. Start praying for ways to reach out to them and bring them back.**

THE STAKES ARE HIGH

We're talking about going and getting wanderers—those who've wandered from the truth and neglected to follow the Lord. And James has been teaching us that it's our responsibility to go get them and bring them back.

We need to understand that God has assigned us this task for a reason. Not because He wants more people in church. Not because He needs more followers to make Him feel important. We go and get the wanderer because every person is important to God, and He doesn't want anyone to perish in their sin (see 2 Pet. 3:9). It's a matter of life or death.

LET THEM KNOW

James continued:

> *My brothers, if anyone among you wanders from the truth*
> *and someone brings him back, let him know that whoever*
> *brings back a sinner from his wandering ...*
> **JAMES 5:19-20**

If **"whoever"** in verse 20 is you, God wants you to know this truth. If you're thinking, *Should I do this?* don't back away. There are some things about seeking wanderers that you need to know.

The stakes are high in bringing back **"a sinner from his wandering" (v. 20).** The New International Version says **"from the error of his way."** Whether that error is the sin itself or the wandering the sin has produced, the fact remains:

> *Whoever brings back a sinner from his wandering*
> *will save his soul from death.*
> **JAMES 5:20**

The stakes couldn't be higher. You're going to save the wanderer's soul from death. What does that mean?

In what way would you save a wanderer from death by bringing him back to the Lord?

James wasn't talking about physical death. We know death is coming for all of us. So obviously, by bringing a wanderer back to the Lord, you're not saving him from physical death.

James was talking about hell. Bringing back a wanderer is going to save him from hell. If you're thinking, *I can't save anyone. That's what God does!* you're absolutely right. One characteristic of an authentic Christian is that he continues in the faith. The writer of the Book of Hebrews warned his readers, recent Jewish converts to Christianity:

> *Take care, brothers, lest there be in any of you an evil, unbelieving heart, leading you to fall away from the living God. For we have come to share in Christ, if indeed we hold our original confidence firm to the end.*
> **HEBREWS 3:12,14**

False professions and fake Christians leave and never come back. True Christians, though they may wander, come back to God.

At this point you may be wondering, *My sister is living outside God's will right now. Is she saved?* We don't know. Here's what we know: if she comes back, she was saved. God may have worked through you to bring her back. The fact that she came back is a confirmation that she was saved or, at the very least, is now saved. If she refuses to return and ultimately dies in that condition, it might indicate that she was never initially saved. In any case, it's not for us to decide whether a wanderer needs salvation or restoration. Our concern is to go get them and bring them home because the stakes are high.

GOD NEVER GIVES UP

Paul wrote:

> *I am sure of this, that he who began a good work in you will bring it to completion at the day of Jesus Christ.*
> **PHILIPPIANS 1:6**

God doesn't give up on any of His children. He may allow them to wander, but He won't leave them there. We go in His name to bring them back. Their return confirms God's commitment to them.

Because the stakes are so high, finding wanderers is a messy business. You can get your feelings hurt and your toes stepped on. You could be called arrogant: "Who do you think you are to tell me anything about my life?" Given these fair warnings, are we selfless enough to risk our own safety and security? God forgive us if we huddle in our holy enclave and don't let Him move our hearts for people who are in danger of eternal consequences.

It's risky business to go after wanderers. You'll feel the weight in your heart. Every person who's out there has built a little house of cards, using all their reasons, rationalizations, explanations, and blame shifting for why they're not in the fold. If you talk to them, you're going to hear all that. Most of them aren't waking up today thinking, *Wow! It really stinks out here in Wanderville. I need to go home.*

But just let them get in a car accident or receive bad news from the doctor. That house of cards will come crashing down, and they'll call out to God. In their heart of hearts, they know what's true. You have to believe He's at work in their lives, softening their hearts and drawing them back to Him.

Even if they reprove or reject you, even if they put you off, mark it down: when they start heading back toward the fold, they'll remember you as the person who cared enough to go to them even when they didn't want to hear the truth.

Think of someone you know who's wandered from the Lord. What risks have you taken or would you be willing to take to go get this wanderer?

What excuses or arguments have you heard him use to keep wandering?

What evidence do you see that God is working in his life?

God never gives up, and neither should you. Go get the wanderers. Show them there's a way back.

DAY 4

THE REWARD IS GREAT

Not only is restoring a wanderer a life-or-death matter, but it also covers sin. James wrote:

My brothers, if anyone among you wanders from the truth and someone brings him back, let him know that whoever brings back a sinner from his wandering will save his soul from death and will cover a multitude of sins.
JAMES 5:19-20

Read the following Scripture verses and record what they teach about the covering of sin.

Psalm 32:1

1 Peter 4:8

COMING HOME TO FORGIVENESS

When you think about what a wanderer might be doing, it can break your heart. But an amazing transformation happens when they come home—when they really come back to the Lord. When wanderers are restored, we don't spend time talking about their sin. It's forgiven.

You're probably familiar with the parable of the prodigal son in Luke 15. We'll study it in-depth in week 5. Do you recall what the father of the prodigal did? He waited and waited for his son, who'd taken his inheritance and squandered it. But when he came home, the father ran to him and gave him a bone-crushing hug. He came home, and all was forgiven. Love covers sin.

Here's a message the wanderer desperately needs to hear. Your past can be forgiven. Your hurts can be healed. Your sin can be atoned for. That's the great truth of the gospel. We celebrate what Jesus has done for sinful people, starting with us. The reward is great.

If you've ever wandered from God and returned to Him, how did you experience His forgiveness?

One of my favorite hymns was written by a man named Robert Robinson. More than a hundred years ago, Robinson composed the great hymn "Come, Thou Fount of Every Blessing." In the second verse he included these lines:

> *Prone to wander, Lord, I feel it,*
> *Prone to leave the God I love.*

Do you ever feel the tendency to wander from God? If so, why?

The story is told that after Robinson wrote that hymn, he walked away from God—for three decades. His proneness to wander became a pattern. Thirty years after his song was published, Robinson met a young woman who happened to be reading a collection of poetry. He was so distraught that he asked her to read to him from her book. She unknowingly read to him the very words of the hymn he had written years before:

> *Prone to wander, Lord, I feel it,*
> *Prone to leave the God I love;*
> *Here's my heart, Lord, take and seal it,*
> *Seal it for Thy courts above.*

Apparently, Robinson not only admitted to having written the lyrics but also to deeply longing to feel again what he'd experienced when God inspired those words. When we sing that hymn, we ask God to seal our hearts against the ever-present human tendency to lose our way. Yet if we wander as Robinson did, we can be sure that God's forgiveness waits for us when we return.

COMING HOME TO CELEBRATION

Another reward of a wanderer's homecoming is great rejoicing. Earlier this week we referred to Jesus' teachings about the lost sheep. Notice the reaction when the sheep were found:

When [the man] has found [the sheep], he lays it on his shoulders, rejoicing. And when he comes home, he calls together his friends and his neighbors, saying to them, "Rejoice with me, for I have found my sheep that was lost."
LUKE 15:5-6

And when the prodigal son returned, his father threw a party for him, celebrating with these words: "My son was dead, and is alive again; he was lost, and is found" (v. 24). God rejoices when a sinner repents and comes home.

RECOGNIZING THE WANDERER

This week you've probably been reminded of wanderers you know. As wanderers come to mind, you might notice that they fit into some of the following categories.

THE PRODIGAL WANDERER. This person's motto is "Nobody tells me what to do. I do what I want to do." Sometimes being a prodigal springs from being young and rebellious. But I've also heard wanderers in their 60s, still willful and stubborn, say, "I want to do *my* thing *my* way."

THE PLEASURE SEEKER. This person isn't willful, just selfish. They want to do what they want when they want, regardless of the consequences. This person has found a particularly tempting sin. The Bible says the "pleasures of sin" (Heb. 11:25) are for a season. They don't last. But this person says, "I'm going to enjoy myself. This makes me happy, and it's what I want to do. I'm having too much fun to worry about what's coming down the road." That's the profile of a pleasure seeker.

THE WOUNDED WANDERER. The wounded wanderer has a story: "I used to go to church. I used to love God. I used to study my Bible." But someone in a position of spiritual authority—maybe a parent or a pastor—hurt, wounded, or disappointed them. Now they're disillusioned with spiritual matters and maybe even blame God.

THE ASHAMED WANDERER. This person lives with a sense of shame over mistakes and sins of the past. Now they feel they can't go back to church and face other Christians. They've fallen, and they can't get up. Part of what makes the church wonderful is that it's filled with people who understand life's detours. Because they know about shame, they offer a loving, safe place where broken people can come. That's because they were once broken themselves.

THE DISTRACTED WANDERER. "Why aren't you at church today?" "Well, I don't know. I couldn't tell you how or when, but God disappeared from my life." Sometimes the distracted wanderers are even at church but not really *there*. The lights are on, but no one's home. Their attention is somewhere else. Ask the distracted wanderer to come to church, and they say, "Sure! Where are we going for lunch afterward?" They're not on task. They just don't get the point. They're not plugged in.

> **Which of these categories best describes a wanderer you have in mind?**

> **Which describes you, either now or at a time in the past?**

No matter what types of wanderers you've identified in your life, God wants you to go get them and bring them home. And He will go with you as you go get the wanderers. They're often just waiting for someone to care.

> **Spend time in prayer preparing to seek a wanderer. Ask God to create a longing and a burden for a wanderer you know or to show you someone you can reach and bring back. Ask for His aid in pursuing this ministry that's close to His heart.**

DAY 5
BRINGING THE WANDERER HOME

This week we've examined James 5:19-20, which clearly tells us to go get those who wander from the truth. I'm sure one or more wanderers came to mind as you studied this week, and I'm excited for you to go and get them.

Day 5 in each week will guide you to bring together your thoughts about the wanderers who've come to mind as you've studied. Your day 5 activities should help you create a plan for going to get the wanderers, as well as encourage and embolden you to put your plan into action.

THE PROBLEM EXISTS

As you completed days 1–4, you probably thought of at least one wanderer.

Record a list of all the people in your life whom you'd consider to be wanderers. You'll refer back to this list throughout the study.

Beside the names, record why you consider each a wanderer. (There may be a different reason for each person.)

Wandering starts with a single step. Do you know someone who seems to be taking steps toward wandering? What makes you think they're headed that way?

What do you think it will require to go and bring these wanderers home?

THERE IS A REMEDY

No one is beyond the reach of God's grace. He invites the wanderers back and celebrates when they return. He promises to save the soul of the returned wanderer in James 5:20, but they need someone to go get them.

How can you demonstrate God's grace and forgiveness to the wanderers in your life?

What steps can you take today to make contact with the wanderers in your life? Suggestions include writing a note, making a phone call, inviting them for coffee, or simply asking how they're doing.

THE STAKES ARE HIGH, BUT THE REWARD IS GREAT

Going to get the wanderer won't be easy or fun. It may cause you discomfort. Your feelings might get hurt. You risk offending or alienating the wanderer for a season. Going to get the wanderer may mean showing God's love to someone who's difficult to love. It may mean acting selflessly for the sake of someone who's selfish. It may mean having faith in the midst of doubters. It might be messy.

However, the reward is worth it. James 5:20 says God will save the wanderer's soul from death. That's not a small matter. That's worth all the discomfort, hurt, pain, and mess involved in going to get the wanderer.

Identify an action you'll take to reach out to a wanderer this week.

PRAY FOR THE WANDERER

Spend time in prayer as you prepare to seek opportunities to go get the wanderers God has laid on your heart this week. Try writing your prayers so that you can refer back to them throughout this study.

> **Pray for wisdom as you look for those who've lost their way. Pray for discernment to know how to demonstrate God's grace and forgiveness to them. Pray for boldness to seize opportunities to go get the wanderers.**

> **Pray for strength and patience as you take risks for the sake of wanderers. Pray for the Holy Spirit to empower you as you wade into messy situations to go get the ones who've wandered from the truth.**

Throughout this week you've been thinking about those you know who are wandering from God or who are taking the first steps of wandering. You've prayed for your role in bringing back the wanderer. Now pray for the wanderers.

> **Refer to your list of the wanderers in your life and spend time praying for each of them.**

Through the rest of this study, regularly refer to this list to pray and think of opportunities you may have to bring the wanderers home.

FEARFUL WANDERER, COME HOME

START

WELCOME BACK TO THIS GROUP DISCUSSION OF *COME HOME.*

The previous group session's application activity invited you to be aware of wanderers in your life and ask God to show you ways you can help bring him or her back to Him. If you're comfortable, share any insights the Lord gave you.

Describe what you liked best about the lessons in week 1. What questions do you have?

What rewards await wanderers who come home?

What hope would you like to share with a wanderer you know?

Today's study will focus on the fearful wanderer. What kinds of fear might keep a wanderer from coming back to God?

To prepare for the DVD segment, read aloud the following verses.

> *Jesus said to them, "You will all fall away because of me this night. For it is written, 'I will strike the shepherd, and the sheep of the flock will be scattered.'" Peter answered him, "Though they all fall away because of you, I will never fall away." Jesus said to him, "Truly, I tell you, this very night, before the rooster crows, you will deny me three times." Peter said to him, "Even if I must die with you, I will not deny you!" And all the disciples said the same.*
> **MATTHEW 26:31,33-35**

WATCH

COMPLETE THE VIEWER GUIDE BELOW AS YOU WATCH DVD SESSION 2.

THE FEARFUL WANDERER

1. He told me, but I didn't _____.

Why a wanderer refuses to listen:

• _____: they don't know, and they're too slow to _____.

Immaturity is the inability to connect actions and _____.

• _____: my will, my thrill, you _____.

• _____: hidden hurts close _____.

• _____: peers in the ears block _____.

2. Now I'm _____ **by what I've done.**

Shame: the painful feeling arising from the realization that personal actions have brought _____

Shame brings the wanderer _____.

3. Now I'm afraid to _____ _____.

_____ shatters shame.

Your fear of coming home is _____.

JESUS' RESPONSE TO A FEARFUL WANDERER

• He lovingly _____ the wanderer.

• He patiently _____ to speak.

• He calls for a clear _____.

• He assures that _____ is possible.

• He insists on true _____.

• He keeps the focus _____.

DISCUSS THE DVD SEGMENT WITH YOUR GROUP, USING THE QUESTIONS BELOW.

What's something new you learned from James's teaching about Peter, the fearful wanderer?

What are some reasons a wanderer refuses to listen to the truth? How do you see these factors at work in the wanderers you know?

Why are wanderers afraid to come home?

What is shame?

Discuss James's statement: "Shame is what brings the wanderer home."

How does repentance shatter shame?

In what sense is the fear of coming back to God irrational?

Identify the ways Jesus pursued and restored Peter. What can you learn from Jesus' approach in order to pursue and bring back the wanderers you know?

Application. This week record past sources of fear and shame in your life as a way of better understanding the fear and shame wanderers feel. Describe how repentance and Jesus' love shattered your fear and shame. Be prepared to talk about your thoughts during the next group session.

This week's Scripture memory.

> *There is no fear in love, but perfect love casts out fear. For fear has to do with punishment, and whoever fears has not been perfected in love.*
> **1 JOHN 4:18**

Assignment. Read week 2 and complete the activities before the next group experience. Consider going deeper into this content by reading chapter 2 in James MacDonald's book *Come Home* (Moody Publishers, 2013).

FEARFUL WANDERER, COME HOME

Not long ago I bought a motorcycle. Some might call it a Hog, but it's more like a horse. People have approached me with worried looks on their faces and asked, "Aren't you known for going too fast?" But here's the truth: I'm so scared on this motorcycle that I err on the side of slow. I know if I stop being scared, I'll actually put myself in danger.

I realize from experience that huge hazards await the overconfident. Scripture says:

> Let anyone who thinks that he stands take heed lest he fall.
> **1 CORINTHIANS 10:12**

The person who thinks, *I'll never wander or struggle; I won't fall; I can handle this* is the person who's really in danger of crashing.

That was the apostle Peter's problem. In Matthew 26 he boasted to Jesus that he'd never let Him down. But just a few hours later, Peter denied ever knowing Him. At that point Peter became a fearful wanderer, too ashamed to come back and seek restitution.

Thankfully, Scripture records the gracious, loving way our Savior restored Peter. That's what He wants to do for every fearful wanderer.

DAY 1

THE FEARFUL WANDERER

As we discovered in week 1, James 5:19-20 supplies us with a compelling invitation to identify and bring back the wanderers we meet:

> *My brothers, if anyone among you wanders from the truth and someone brings him back, let him know that whoever brings back a sinner from his wandering will save his soul from death and will cover a multitude of sins.*
> **JAMES 5:19-20**

Why do so many people turn away? I believe many times they don't mean to leave. They just wake up one day thinking, *What am I doing here? This isn't what I wanted for my life.*

If you've ever wandered from the Lord, describe the way it happened.

What led you back to God?

PETER, THE WANDERER

Even Peter, one of the disciples, wandered. If someone who shadowed Jesus for three years could get off track and find himself in a bad place, who are we to say it couldn't happen to us or to someone close to us?

To identify the danger of wandering, let's trace Peter's story, starting in Matthew 26. This was the final week leading up to Jesus' crucifixion. It began with the triumphal entry, and the disciples felt that Jesus' rise to power was imminent.

Then Passover came, and they gathered for the Last Supper in the upper room. Judas's betrayal had been foretold and began to unfold. Matthew briefly summarizes the meal and Jesus' introduction of the Lord's Supper. Then Jesus and His disciples went to the Mount of Olives, where Jesus made a stunningly clear prediction: **"You will all fall away because of me this night" (v. 31).**

What would have been an appropriate response when Jesus said to Peter and the others, "You're going to fall away from Me"? Any one of them could have said, "Lord, I don't want to do that! You know everything, so I have to take this very seriously. But I don't want to fall away. How can we keep this from happening?"

You'd think at least *one* of the eleven would have humbled himself (Judas had bailed out by then). But none of them did. In fact, Peter answered, **"Though they all fall away because of you, I will never fall away" (v. 33).**

Notice the blinding nature of overconfidence. When you're brashly optimistic about something, you're in great danger. Peter was blinded to his own weakness because he was so impulsively sure of himself.

> **Describe a time when you were overconfident about your spiritual strength. What was the result?**

Jesus didn't rebuke Peter. He wasn't harsh or angry with him, but He was firm and clear:

> *Jesus said to him, "Truly, I tell you, this very night, before the rooster crows, you will deny me three times."*
> **MATTHEW 26:34**

The Lord said Peter would deny Him, not once but three times. Did Peter get it? Did he cry out to Jesus, "Lord, help me! I don't want to do this!"? No, he dug in deeper:

> *Peter said to him, "Even if I must die with you, I will not deny you!" And all the disciples said the same.*
> **MATTHEW 26:35**

The others followed Peter's lead—right off the cliff of overconfidence.

That exchange concerns me when I think about the way you and I respond to God. Peter talked boldly, thinking he was ready to stand for Christ. He felt confident that he was totally right but that Jesus was dead wrong. When Peter found himself disagreeing with the Son of God, you might have thought he'd stop talking and start listening. But Peter was completely blind to his own spiritual weakness and to his need to depend on God.

In retrospect Peter might have said, "He told me, but I didn't listen." That's the testimony of every wanderer.

REASONS A WANDERER REFUSES TO LISTEN

Why do wanderers refuse to listen? Why do they ignore warnings about the consequences of wandering from God? Here are some reasons.

IMMATURITY. The immature don't know, and they're slow to grow. They don't recognize their immaturity, so they're not ready to learn yet. Immaturity is the inability to connect actions and consequences. Immature people don't understand that when they take this action, they get that reaction or result. They can't make the connection between their choices and what comes because of their actions. That's immaturity. Immature people need to discover the unbreakable law of cause and effect that God has established in the universe. You choose to sin; you choose to suffer.

How have you experienced the truth of "You choose to sin; you choose to suffer"?

REBELLION. "My will. My thrill. You chill." Those are the proud declarations of rebellion. "No one's going to get between my will and my thrill! This is what *I* want to do. You back off!" They won't listen, and they try to cut off others' attempts to help. They're rebels stuck in overdrive, headed for a wall—and they don't care!

WOUNDEDNESS. Hidden hurts close hearts and ears. "Why doesn't she listen to me more?" She could be wounded. Something may have happened that left unseen scars. Sometimes in a family, even in a church family, things happen that few people know about. Wounded wanderers hold it all inside instead of dealing with it. They're hurting, but they don't bring it out in the open. They're not listening to reason because they have a hidden wound.

PEER PRESSURE. When we're trying to impress others, things we should be afraid of don't register. I can remember, to my own shame, being about 18 years old, cruising in my father's 455-horse, four-barrel carburetor Oldsmobile. I was traveling 90 miles an hour on a country road. Then I hit the gas and felt the engine open up and *vvvrrrroooom*— I felt the need for speed!

"Were you crazy?" The answer is yes. My actions were absolutely, insanely foolish. You ask, "How could you be so stupid?" There were a lot of reasons for my decisions, but the main one was a friend of mine in the passenger seat shouting, "Go! Go! Go!"

I should have been terrified, but peers in the ears block fears. There are many times we should be afraid, but we aren't because we're more concerned about impressing our friends and the people around us. It's a very dangerous place for a wanderer to be.

Identify a time when one of the previous factors kept you from listening to a warning about the way you were living. What happened?

Which of these signs have you seen in a wanderer you know?

Three of those reasons probably contributed to Peter's failure to heed Jesus' warning that night. Peter was probably immature in his faith, judging by the other impulsive things he said and did. Rebellion may have been a contributing factor; Peter and the other disciples were ready for Jesus to rise up and overthrow their Roman oppressors. And Peter was probably under peer pressure since he no doubt wanted to boast in front of the other disciples.

You may see these same reasons at work in the wanderers you encounter—or maybe in yourself. A fearful wanderer who won't listen is in grave danger. But this week we'll see how Jesus responds to fearful wanderers like Peter to bring them back to Him.

DAY 2

WHEN A WANDERER DOESN'T LISTEN

This week we're looking at the story of Peter to understand fearful wanderers. Hopefully, you'll see some patterns in Peter's behavior that you'll recognize in wanderers you know.

Yesterday we saw Jesus warn Peter that he'd fall away from faithfulness to his Lord. In fact, He said Peter would deny Him three times. Yet Peter wouldn't listen, claiming he'd never deny Jesus (see Matt. 26:35).

UNMASKED AND ASHAMED

In the garden of Gethsemane Jesus asked Peter, James, and John to watch and pray with Him, but they couldn't stay awake (see vv. 36-46). Let's pick up the account after Jesus' arrest. Peter was cautiously following the Roman guard and the crowd that was escorting Jesus (see v. 58). Peter was tracking from a distance. John, who was also following, arranged for Peter to get into the high priest's courtyard, or the big fisherman would have been left out on the street (see John 18:15-16). Read what happened next:

> *Peter was sitting outside in the courtyard. And a servant girl came up to him and said, "You also were with Jesus the Galilean." But he denied it before them all, saying, "I do not know what you mean." And when he went out to the entrance, another servant girl saw him, and she said to the bystanders, "This man was with Jesus of Nazareth." And again he denied it with an oath: "I do not know the man." After a little while the bystanders came up and said to Peter, "Certainly you too are one of them, for your accent betrays you." Then he began to invoke a curse on himself and to swear, "I do not know the man." And immediately the rooster crowed. And Peter remembered the saying of Jesus, "Before the rooster crows, you will deny me three times." And he went out and wept bitterly.*
> **MATTHEW 26:69-75**

Why do you think Peter denied Jesus?

When questioned, Peter completely forgot about his earlier boast that he'd never deny Jesus. His first response was **"I do not know what you mean" (v. 70).** We call that playing dumb. He was deflecting the obvious truth. Things were getting uncomfortable.

Next Peter used a curse, an expletive, to emphatically say, **"I do not know the man"** (v. 72). You don't know Him, Peter? You don't know the One who called you? You don't know the One who dubbed you the Rock, whom you saw feed five thousand people? He was transfigured before you. You don't *know* Him, Peter?

Later a group of people approached him. When someone in the crowd pressed Peter further, he began to swear, saying something like "I'd rather burn in hell than be in the company of that guy!" Wow! You were going to die for Him, Peter? Were you a little overconfident earlier?

Then the rooster crowed, and Peter remembered Jesus' prediction. This is one of the saddest phrases in the Bible: **"He went out and wept bitterly" (v. 75).** Luke 22:61 tells us when the rooster crowed, Peter was within view of the Lord, maybe 50 yards away. They made eye contact. Peter saw Jesus right after his third denial while the crowing echoed in his ears. Then he turned and fled, weeping bitterly. The Greek word translated *bitterly* means *violent, uncontrolled, convulsing sobs*. The sobs came in scalding waves of shame and disappointment, the wordless groans of a broken man. Head bowed, shoulders heaving, Peter was a picture of shame.

> **Have you ever been unmasked and ashamed like Peter, hidden in a falsehood one moment, then suddenly exposed the next? Describe the incident.**

> **How did you respond to your shame?**

Being ashamed isn't always a bad thing. People sometimes say, "You don't ever want to feel shame." In trying to increase self-esteem, our society has promoted shamelessness without acknowledging the fact that sometimes our behavior *should* make us ashamed. Shame can be a good thing. When you lose your capacity to feel shame, you're in a very dangerous place.

Shame can be defined as *the painful feeling arising from a realization that personal actions have brought disgrace*. Shame is the acknowledgment that what you did revealed truth about you and cast a negative light on others as well as on yourself. Shame can get a wanderer's attention and turn him back toward home.

Think of a wanderer you've been praying for. What has he done to be ashamed of?

How can God use that shame to help the wanderer recognize his need for God?

RESPONDING TO SHAME

We've all done something we're ashamed of. Shame is a shared human experience, a natural response of the human conscience to wrongdoing. The problem is that people often handle shame in harmful ways. When you're ashamed of something you've done, how do you deal with the disgrace? If you deal with it in unhealthy ways, you develop destructive behaviors that can compound the shame and devastate your life.

Let's look at some destructive responses to shame so that you can recognize these in the fearful wanderers you encounter.

DENYING SHAME. You just block out the shame, thinking, *If I can no longer see it, it didn't happen*. For example, if you were abused as a child, you just deny the shame and say to yourself, *It didn't happen. It's not a problem*. When you deny shame, you bury it deep inside you, but it spreads like a cancer in your soul.

DILUTING SHAME. You minimize the shame. That's what Adam and Eve did after eating the fruit in Genesis 3. They tried to cover their shame by hiding from God (see v. 8), but that just drove them away from the only One who could help. When you dilute shame, you often perpetuate that behavior. That's why so many people who were abused go on to become abusers. They don't want to be alone with their feelings, so they add others to the circle of shame.

DESPAIRING IN SHAME. "I can't take this. I can't be this person. I can't face another day." Satan wants to push us to that extreme. That's the way Judas dealt with his shame—by taking his life (see Matt. 27:5). Reaching a point of despair is an awful, self-destructive way to deal with shame.

DEPARTING FROM SHAME. Some people flee the scene, hoping to get as far away from the source and reminders of shame as possible. Peter used this tactic when he left the chief priest's courtyard in tears over his shameful behavior.

> **Think of the wanderers you know. Identify ways they're—**
>
> **denying shame:**
>
>
> **diluting shame:**
>
>
> **despairing in shame:**
>
>
> **departing from shame:**
>
>
> **Have you ever used one of those tactics to deal with shame? Briefly describe what happened.**

Tomorrow we'll see that Peter's instinctive response to flee didn't work out great for him. But the fact that his overconfidence and pride had been broken would open his heart to change and restoration. Jesus wasn't through with this fearful wanderer.

DAY 3
AFRAID TO COME HOME

When we last saw Peter, he was in bad shape. No sooner had he denied his Lord than the rooster crowed, and he realized what he'd done. He left the chief priest's courtyard completely ashamed, no longer the boastful disciple we saw before Jesus' arrest.

Yet Jesus wasn't finished with Peter. There were numerous postresurrection appearances by Jesus, but this one changed everything for Peter. Let's take up his story in John 21:

> *After this Jesus revealed himself again to the disciples by the Sea of Tiberias, and he revealed himself in this way. Simon Peter, Thomas (called the Twin), Nathanael of Cana in Galilee, the sons of Zebedee, and two others of his disciples were together. Simon Peter said to them, "I am going fishing."*
> **JOHN 21:1-3**

Peter told the other disciples, **"I am going fishing" (v. 3).** He went back to what he'd done before Jesus called him. It was a big step backward from being a fisher of men to being a fisherman again.

Peter's experience may speak to a wanderer you know. Jesus warned Peter, but he didn't listen. He insisted that he knew better than Jesus did. Ashamed by what he'd done, Peter was now afraid to come home.

REPENTANCE SHATTERS SHAME

Peter is an example of how *not* to deal with shame. You don't have to live in your sin. You don't have to wallow in the mire of your failure. You can be washed. You can be cleansed. You can repent and be forgiven. You can have a fresh start. You can have your whole life turned around. Jesus frees us from our shame.

Instead of running away, Peter should have fallen to his knees and said, "I'm wrong. I've been wrong all along. It's all my fault. I have no one to blame but myself." He should have leaned into the Lord's grace and forgiveness. He should have run to His arms and found the forgiveness and cleansing he so desperately needed. Only repentance shatters shame.

Grace was right there for Peter, but he wouldn't embrace it. He ran from it. He thought Jesus was the problem when He was really the solution. So Peter said, **"I am going fishing."** How sad. How painful. He could have shattered his shame with repentance, but he supersized it by running and hiding. He was afraid to come home.

Describe a time when you didn't want to come home because of shame. Did you choose to repent or run away?

So there's Peter, filled with shame, floating on a dark sea. John 21 records how quickly he returned to an old, familiar pattern:

They went out and got into the boat, but that night they caught nothing.
JOHN 21:3

Don't you think that's an awesome miracle? They didn't catch *anything*. That's a miracle. These guys were fishermen. They knew the hot spots on the lake. They knew how to cast the nets. This wasn't fishing with a pole and lure, casting all night without a bite. They were throwing big nets weighted with rocks out across the water and pulling them in. When the Bible says they caught nothing, it means the nets were empty every time. They didn't see a single tuna, tilapia, mackerel, minnow, or starfish. It's a miracle.

That's what God always does when we're wandering. He brings our efforts to futility and then speaks into our frustrations: "Coming up empty again? It's not what you thought it would be? Humble yourself and return, running to the One who loves you, who will forgive you, and who will wash your heart clean." Hear His whisper, humble yourself, and come home.

Describe a time when repentance led you to restoration with God.

FACING FEAR

Like Peter, maybe you're afraid to come home, or maybe you're thinking of a wanderer you know who's afraid to come home. The truth is that your fear is irrational. If you examine it, that fear won't make sense. Fear is a false barrier holding you back.

A wanderer thinks, *If I go home, I'm going to get an earful. If I come back to the Lord and back to church, everyone's going to look down on me. They're going to make me feel awful and filthy.*

That's an irrational fear. It's not the way it really is. As the body of Christ, we love you. We've been praying for you. We've been waiting for you. And God has been waiting for you. Jesus said:

> *There will be more joy in heaven over one sinner who repents than over ninety-nine righteous persons who need no repentance.*
> **LUKE 15:7**

Your return is the moment we're all waiting for.

I'm reminded of the biblical account of David and Bathsheba. King David saw this woman, took her, and then had her husband killed in battle. That's a lot to be ashamed of, but when confronted with his sin, David immediately repented: "I have sinned against the LORD" (2 Sam. 12:13). In Scripture we have a psalm that records David's confession and prayer of repentance.

Read Psalm 51. What words indicate that David recognized his sin?

What requests indicate that David truly sought repentance?

Unlike Peter, David faced up to his sin right away, realizing that having forgiveness and restored fellowship with God outweighed any fear about coming into God's presence.

Being afraid to come home is irrational. Why? Because we're coming home to Jesus. Being with Him is so much better than hanging back in our shame. That's something Peter was about to learn. And it's something the wanderers in your life need to hear.

As you pray for the wanderers you know, pray that they'll hunger to be restored to God and that you'll be able to show them that the benefits of coming home far outweigh their fears.

JESUS RESTORES THE FEARFUL WANDERER

Let's look at the way Jesus responded to Peter, the wanderer, to learn how He can restore the wanderers you're acquainted with. John 21:4 tells us, **"Just as day was breaking, Jesus stood on the shore."**

I'm tremendously comforted by Jesus' presence on the shore of any place in my life. It's a reminder that Jesus lovingly pursues the wanderer.

JESUS LOVINGLY PURSUES THE WANDERER

Jesus stood on the shore and waited until the time was right, then shouted in the morning light, "You guys haven't caught any fish, have you?" If you read this question with a tone of reproof, you've missed Jesus' spirit. He must have been smiling in anticipation of what He was about to do *for* them and *to* them. He asked them, **"Children, do you have any fish?" (v. 5),** to which they answered no in unison. They didn't recognize Him yet.

When Jesus told the disciples to cast their nets on the other side of the boat, they got an enormous, miraculous catch. Then they recognized Jesus, and Peter jumped into the water and rushed to shore—the best decision he had made in a long time. They counted the fish and cleaned a few for breakfast. Jesus broke bread and gave it to them in verse 13. Just like old times again, on the road with Jesus.

Let me ask you several questions. Has Jesus been pursuing you? Do you strive to avoid truth and truth tellers through whom His Spirit can speak to you? Do you fear time alone when His Spirit can corner you and really talk to you about where you are? Do you secretly long for peace but fear the journey to a better place? Do you find right now that you're squirming because you know you're not where you've wanted to be?

> **If you answered yes to any of those questions, thank God for lovingly pursuing you. Ask Him to help you submit to His desire to bring you home.**

Let the Lord speak to your heart today. Hear the message that the fearful wanderer can come home. He lovingly pursues you.

JESUS PATIENTLY WAITS TO SPEAK

I wish I had understood the value of patience earlier in my life. I've always been someone who thinks, *It needs to be said. I'm going to say it now.* I have to acknowledge that Jesus wasn't hurried or impatient. He chose His time to talk to Peter.

Jesus could have immediately confronted Peter when He first appeared to the disciples. He could have addressed the elephant-in-the-room issue immediately: "Before we get into anything, Peter, we need to talk. Here's a hint: cock-a-doodle-doo! Could've *died* for Me, huh? What's up now?" Jesus did nothing like that with Peter.

Someone may have treated you that way, but that's not the Lord. Multiple times Jesus had a chance to challenge Peter, but He never spoke about their situation until this morning on the seashore. And when He spoke to him, He waited all night while they were fishing and catching nothing, waited while they came to shore, waited all through the whole breakfast as He served them. He waited for the right time to talk to Peter.

> **Describe an occasion when Jesus spoke to you at just the right time to bring you back to Him.**

JESUS CALLS FOR A CLEAR DECISION

Jesus didn't give Peter a big speech or a lecture. He didn't rehearse his past. Just this:

> *When they had finished breakfast, Jesus said to Simon Peter, "Simon, son of John, do you love me more than these?"*
> **JOHN 21:15**

More than these what? More than these fish and the life they represented. There were 153 fish in the net (see v. 11). That was Peter's old life. That wasn't the person he was supposed to be anymore. Jesus pulled Peter aside for a crucial question because the time was exactly right: "Peter, do you love Me more than these—this life I've called you from, this thing that was never so great for you, even this shame you're carrying? Do you love Me more than this?"

Notice that Jesus called him **"Simon, son of John" (v. 15)**. His nickname was Peter; Jesus always called him Peter—that's the name He gave him. But this moment was more serious than a nickname. It's like the way we talk to our kids. When I call my first son Luke James MacDonald, he knows it's time for a serious talk. This isn't going to be nice chat. "Do you know who you are, Simon? I know who you are. I know it *all*. It's time to get back to your identity, Peter—who you really are." I love the way Jesus has done that for me, and I know He will do it for you.

How has Jesus called you to a new life with Him?

JESUS ASSURES THAT PURPOSE IS POSSIBLE

Peter responded to Jesus, **"Yes, Lord; you know that I love you" (v. 15)**. Peter was expressing caution learned from failure. Weeks before he would have blurted, "Absolutely, Lord. You can count on me." Now he was hoping Jesus would find his faith true.

Jesus replied, **"Feed my lambs" (v. 15)**. Peter must have wondered how Jesus could trust him with anything after he denied Him three times. But Jesus was saying, "It's all right, Peter. You did it. You blew it. But the past is over. I'm not done with you yet."

Now that's grace. When Jesus shows up, He assures us that purpose in our lives is possible. That's a good word for you today. Receive that hopeful message. God isn't done with you yet. It's not too late for you, wanderer.

How has God shown you lately that He has a purpose for your life?

JESUS INSISTS ON TRUE COMMITMENT

Not once but three times Jesus asked, **"Simon, do you love Me?"** And Peter had to answer three times:

> *Yes, Lord; you know that I love you. ... Yes, Lord; you know that I love you. ... Lord, you know everything; you know that I love you.*
> **JOHN 21:15-17**

The exchange was awkward but necessary. So why did Jesus ask three times? Not long ago Peter had denied the Lord three times. So Jesus used three questions to call Peter to a true commitment and restoration.

How can love for Jesus play a role in bringing a wanderer home?

Peter's answers point the way for every wanderer: "Lord, I can't deny it. I do love You. It's what I really want. I didn't want to stay where I wandered away. I was too prideful. I was too self-confident. Now I know how wrong I was."

Church history records that in about A.D. 65 Peter was executed in Rome under orders from Nero. He had a great life of serving God, but he had a tough finish.

Following Christ isn't easy. The Christian life isn't always smooth going, but it's exactly what we were designed to do and be. It's the real life. It's the best life you can possibly have: giving your life to Jesus Christ, living for Him, obeying His Word, fellowshipping with His people, and serving in His kingdom. Come home to that life.

Scripture describes God as:

> *Merciful and gracious, slow to anger, and abounding in steadfast love and faithfulness.*
> **EXODUS 34:6**

The fearful wanderer needs to know there's nothing to fear. There's a loving, safe place with God's children in the presence of Christ.

Write a truth from today's lesson that you'd like to share with a wanderer.

Pray that wanderers you know will cast aside their fear, humble themselves, confess their failures, and receive God's forgiveness. Ask God for opportunities to help these wanderers come home.

What about you? Is there a sin you've been afraid to confess? Let your love for Christ bring you back home to God and a renewed commitment to Him. Repent and ask Him to restore your fellowship with Him.

DAY 5

BRINGING THE WANDERER HOME

I'm sure you can think of times when you wandered from God the way Peter did. It happens when we're overconfident and refuse to listen. Maybe someone you know accurately fits the description of a fearful wanderer. Jesus demonstrated in John 21 how we should respond to fearful wanderers. Peter came back, and so can the wanderers we know and love.

> Look back in week 1, day 5 at your list of the wanderers in your life. Identify any who fit the description of a fearful wanderer. Keep them in mind as you complete today's lesson.

WHEN THE WANDERER DOESN'T LISTEN

In day 1 I outlined several reasons wanderers may not listen to the truth. They may be immature, rebellious, wounded, or pressured by those around them.

> What are some ways you can demonstrate the truth of Christ to a wanderer who refuses to listen?

> Read 1 Peter 3:13-17. What encouragement does this passage give you as you share truth with those who may not listen?

> Verse 15 says to share hope "with gentleness and respect." What does that look like for a wanderer?

GRACE FOR SHAME

Fearful wanderers are often filled with shame when they recognize they've wandered from the truth. They're in pain because they realize they've hurt themselves, Christ, and people they love. Shame can be a good thing, but it can lead to some bad responses. When we welcome back a fearful wanderer, we must be ready to forgive.

> Read Colossians 3:12-15. What do these verses say about the way we should respond to wanderers—both those who are returning and those who are still wandering?

> What does it mean to give grace to those who've wandered? To those still wandering?

A CHRISTLIKE RESPONSE TO THE FEARFUL WANDERER

Jesus' response to Peter gives us an example of how we can go get the fearful wanderers in our lives.

LOVINGLY PURSUE. Jesus didn't leave Peter alone. He went after Him (see John 21:4). He was there when Peter was ready to return to Him.

> How can you lovingly pursue a wanderer who isn't ready to come back?

> What are some practical ways you can demonstrate to the wanderers in your life that you're ready to welcome them back? How will you show them this week?

PATIENTLY WAIT TO SPEAK. Jesus didn't confront Peter with his wandering right away. He waited until the right time to talk with Peter.

Read 1 Peter 3:15 again. Why do you think Peter said to always be prepared to make a defense? How do you think that relates to patiently waiting to speak to a wanderer?

Pray for wisdom in determining when to stay silent and when to speak truth into the wanderer's life.

CALL FOR A CLEAR DECISION. Wanderers need you to speak truthfully to them. While we should do it gently and respectfully (see 1 Pet. 3:15), we also shouldn't shy away from the truth of the gospel.

Do you know the truth of the gospel? Do you have a defense for "anyone who asks you for a reason for the hope that is in you" (1 Pet. 3:15)? Write your defense and practice it so that you'll be ready to defend the truth.

What is the clear decision you need to call for in a particular wanderer's life? How can you do that with gentleness and respect?

ASSURE THE WANDERER THAT PURPOSE IS POSSIBLE. Wanderers often feel that hope is lost. They've messed up and may feel God can no longer use them because of their mistakes. When we go get wanderers, we need to assure them it's not too late. After coming back from wandering, Peter went on to lead the early church and to write two books of the New Testament. If God could use Peter, He can still use the wanderers in your life.

What are some ways God can use wanderers to glorify Himself?

How can you demonstrate to a wanderer you know that it's not too late?

INSIST ON TRUE COMMITMENT. When Jesus brought Peter back, He didn't shy away from asking him to make a commitment (see John 21:15-17). In the same way, we need to ask our wanderer to make a full commitment to Christ. No more wandering. No more fear.

What would it look like for a wanderer you know to make a true commitment to God?

How would you call a wanderer you know to make such a commitment?

PRAY FOR THE FEARFUL WANDERER

Pray that fearful wanderers you know will come to a point of frustration with their running and wandering and be ready to listen to the truth. Pray that they'll find grace, hope, and love with God and His people. Ask that they'll see you as a friend who's pursuing them in love. Pray that they'll be ready to make an initial or renewed commitment to follow Christ.

DOUBTFUL WANDERER, COME HOME

START

WELCOME BACK TO THIS GROUP
DISCUSSION OF *COME HOME.*

The previous group session's application activity asked you to record
past sources of fear and shame in your life and to describe how
repentance and Jesus' love shattered your fear and shame. If you're
comfortable, share ways this activity has helped you understand the
fear and shame wanderers experience.

Describe what you liked best about the lessons in week 2.
What questions do you have?

How can your church offer a welcoming, forgiving environment
for wanderers who are ashamed of what they've done and are fearful
of being judged?

Today's study will focus on the doubtful wanderer. What kinds
of doubts might keep a wanderer from coming back to God?

To prepare for the DVD segment, read aloud the following verses.

> *Thomas, one of the Twelve, called the Twin, was*
> *not with them when Jesus came. So the other*
> *disciples told him, "We have seen the Lord."*
> *But he said to them, "Unless I see in his hands*
> *the mark of the nails, and place my finger into*
> *the mark of the nails, and place my hand into*
> *his side, I will never believe."*
> **JOHN 20:24-25**

WATCH

Sometimes people find it difficult to admit at church that they have _____.

KINDS OF DOUBTERS

1. The empirical doubter: believing would require _____ I don't have.

Areas of attack for the empirical doubter: evidence for the existence of _____,
for _____ versus evolution, for _____, for the reliability and
the miraculous nature of the _____

2. The disillusioned doubter: believing would require _____ I don't see.

God prefers the sincere worship of those who _____ Him to the robotic
worship of the masses.

All of the pain, heartache, and suffering in this world are the result of people not
choosing _____.

3. The disappointed doubter: believing would require _____ I don't desire.

Forgiveness is the decision to release a person from the _____
that resulted when they injured you.

4. The moral doubter: believing would require _____ I don't want.

BUILDING THE FIRE OF FAITH

1. Faith is dead when the heart is _____.

Complaining about persistent doubts, if you are never in the place where faith
is _____, is like complaining about the darkness in your basement under
a blanket with the lights off.

Where faith flourishes: in the _____ of God, in friendship with _____ of faith,
in the _____ of God

2. Faith is kindled when the heart identifies the _____.

God will go a long way in revealing Himself to a person who really wants
to _____.

3. Faith is sparked when the Lord reveals Himself at our point of _____.

4. Faith is ignited when the heart submits to the _____.

5. Faith is ablaze when it comes before _____.

DISCUSS THE DVD SEGMENT WITH YOUR GROUP, USING THE QUESTIONS BELOW.

What's something new you learned from James's teaching about Thomas, the doubtful wanderer?

What types of doubters have you encountered—empirical, disillusioned, disappointed, or moral? What types of conversations have you had with these wanderers?

Have you ever had doubts? What kinds, and how did you resolve them?

Respond to James's statement: "Complaining about persistent doubts, if you are never in the place where faith is built, is like complaining about the darkness in your basement under a blanket with the lights off. If you want faith, you've got to get to the places where faith flourishes."

Where does faith flourish?

Why is it important to identify the obstacles to faith?

How can a fresh encounter with Jesus change a doubter's perspective?

Application. As you go through the week, note times when you find yourself doubting God's character or promises. What kinds of situations provoked these moments of doubt? Conversely, when were you less likely to doubt? Be prepared to talk about your experiences during the next group session.

This week's Scripture memory.

> *Without faith it is impossible to please him, for whoever would draw near to God must believe that he exists and that he rewards those who seek him.*
> **HEBREWS 11:6**

Assignment. Read week 3 and complete the activities before the next group experience. Consider going deeper into this content by reading chapter 3 in James MacDonald's book *Come Home* (Moody Publishers, 2013).

DOUBTFUL WANDERER, COME HOME

Before we launched Harvest Bible Chapel, I was a youth pastor. We used to take our high-school students on a summer trip to Algonquin Park in northern Ontario. The trip involved canoeing and primitive camping in the wilderness—a real adventure for many young people.

One night Kathy and I were asleep in our tent between the girls' camp on one side and the guys' camp on the other. We were awakened by an unusual noise, something moving around outside our tent. I thought for a moment—yes, we'd remembered to raise all our provisions in bags into a tree so that a bear couldn't get them. That meant the only edible things in the camp were us!

I remember lying in my sleeping bag, listening to the creature rooting around outside with only a thin wall of nylon between us. The noise seemed big and loud. I can't think of another time in my life when I was more scared. I pictured a grizzly out there sharpening its claws to work on me. But since I was the big protector of all the students, I had to venture forth, armed with my flashlight. I was trembling as I unzipped the tent and poked my head out … only to see several little raccoons scurry into the darkness. How could such small creatures make such a terrifying noise? Until my eyes corrected what I was hearing, I was filled with fear and doubt.

When you're in the darkness, doubting comes easily. Isolation and blindness heighten doubts and fears. Your mind can get so off track and in such a bad place when you can't see. That's why we must keep God's Word in our hands. It's the light we need to stay focused on the truth and to lead the doubtful wanderer home.

DAY 1
THE DARKNESS OF DOUBT

We're continuing our study of wanderers in Scripture and letting God speak to us about the wanderers in our lives who need to come home. Our foundational Scripture is this passage from James:

> *My brothers, if anyone among you wanders from the truth and someone brings him back, let him know that whoever brings back a sinner from his wandering will save his soul from death and will cover a multitude of sins.*
> **JAMES 5:19-20**

This week we're talking about the doubting wanderer. It's easy to see how doubters wander away from God. Does God exist? Will He do what He says? Does He really care? Is His Word really true? These are legitimate questions for believers to ask, and they can lead to a stronger faith and a greater commitment to God. But if these kinds of questions go unresolved, they can eventually undermine our faith and lead us away from the truth.

Doubts need to be settled. Maybe that word *doubtful* in this week's title immediately struck a chord in you: "That's me. I can't move because I doubt. I'm stuck. How do I get past these nagging uncertainties? Can they really be settled?"

John 20 tells the story of one of Jesus' disciples who, after the resurrection, had a hard time believing his fellow disciples had seen the Lord alive. He was hampered by doubts:

> *Thomas, one of the Twelve, called the Twin, was not with them when Jesus came. So the other disciples told him, "We have seen the Lord." But he said to them, "Unless I see in his hands the mark of the nails, and place my finger into the mark of the nails, and place my hand into His side, I will never believe."*
> **JOHN 20:24-25**

Can you identify with Thomas in this passage? If so, in what ways?

Where does doubt most often crop up in your Christian walk?

Using Thomas as our guide, let's look more closely at doubters. By observing the way Jesus dealt with Thomas's doubts, we can learn how to help the doubtful wanderers in our lives.

KINDS OF DOUBTERS

All doubting isn't created equal. Different factors trigger doubt in people's lives. If you're going to bring back doubting wanderers, you need to understand what fuels their doubts.

Today we'll examine the empirical doubter. An empirical doubter is a scholar, a student, or an ntellectual who says in effect, "Believing would require information I don't have. I've got questions. I have issues. I see problems. I need more information, or I won't be able to believe in God, in His Word, or in the gospel."

Empirical doubters aren't a modern phenomenon. Some of them are honest; some aren't. Both kinds show up in the Bible. When Pilate asked Jesus, "What is truth?" (John 18:38), he was playing the role of an empirical doubter, but he wasn't really seeking the truth. When a recently healed blind man asked Jesus, "Who is he [the Son of Man], sir, that I may believe in him?" (John 9:36), he was expressing his willingness to believe, at the same time needing a little more information.

Have you ever talked with empirical doubters? If so, what areas of doubt did they raise?

Because we can't always determine when a doubter's response is honest and when it's an effort to avoid the need for faith, here are some areas where we must be prepared to give an answer when doubters raise questions as an explanation for their uncertainty. Each of these can be reasonably answered for an honest doubter.

EVIDENCE FOR THE EXISTENCE OF GOD. Empirical doubters often say, "I'm not even sure if there really *is* a God. How do I know if there's a God?" In the most basic philosophical thought, you really have just two choices in settling that question: either you believe there's an unknown (or perhaps knowable) cause of the universe called God, or you believe all we see came from no cause at all.

Read the following verses and record evidence for the existence of God.

Psalm 19:1

Ecclesiastes 3:11

What evidence could you present to a doubter about the existence of God?

EVIDENCE FOR CREATION VERSUS EVOLUTION. Probably the greatest single act of villainy in modern scholarship is the perpetuation of evolution taught as fact when it's only a theory. The offense can be found everywhere in the educational system. So much could be said about the real problems with the theory. But just the gaps in the fossil records by themselves almost negate the theory of evolution.

Some claim that intelligent design is also just a theory. I agree, but it's a theory based on evidence. As I examine and question the evidence, there are rational reasons for believing design came from a Designer.

EVIDENCE FOR MIRACLES. Science is famous for claiming there can't be miracles because they aren't repeatable and observable. In science empirical certainty is attained by the proof of repetition. That's a matter of huge significance in scientific theory. If it doesn't happen as a course of regularity, according to natural law, it's not believable. If it doesn't happen repeatedly and observably, it's not true.

The fact is that when proponents of the Big Bang theory state it as fact, they're violating their own standards because the Big Bang is neither repeatable nor observable. The same is true with an atheist's theory of how life began: "There was this primordial ooze, and it came together with maybe some lightning; we're not sure. And *zap!* There was the first living thing; it came from deadness." Again, it's never been repeated, and it can't be observed, so according to scientific methods, it can't be true. Yet scientists treat it as fact while castigating Christians for believing in miracles.

EVIDENCE FOR THE RESURRECTION OF JESUS CHRIST. The evidence for the truth of Jesus' resurrection, both internal and external to the Bible, is stunning. Almost every generation has produced doubters and skeptics who tried to expose the "real" reason for the empty tomb but who came to the humbling realization of the truth of Jesus' claims and actions. Men like Frank Morison *(Who Moved the Stone?)*, C. S. Lewis *(Mere Christianity* and *Miracles)*, Lee Strobel *(The Case for Christ),* and many others have tried to disprove the resurrection but ended up following the risen Lord.

What evidence of Jesus' resurrection would you offer a doubtful wanderer?

EVIDENCE FOR THE RELIABILITY AND THE MIRACULOUS NATURE OF THE BIBLE. Why do I believe the Bible? I can't go into those matters at great length here, but there are rational reasons I believe the Bible—both internal and external to the Bible. Every follower of Jesus should have in his hands, heart, and mind the evidence for the reliability of Scripture.

ANSWERING AN EMPIRICAL DOUBTER

An empirical doubter claims a lack of information as a barrier to belief. But let me ask, Is it information you don't *have* or information you don't *want?* The truths of Christianity have satisfied the greatest minds in human history. Most of us aren't even capable of framing a question for which Scripture doesn't provide an excellent, satisfying answer. Yet people hold God at a distance with a skeptical pseudointellectualism that perpetuates doubt rather than searching it out and investigating the possibilities.

If you have real questions, there are good answers. God's skin isn't so thin that an honest skeptic needs to be fearful of asking the wrong questions. Present your questions and get good answers.

If you're an intellectual doubter, you also have to ask yourself the question, Is it that I don't *have* the answers or that I don't *want* the answers? Because the answers are available, and they'll satisfy the good mind God has given to you.

If you know empirical wanderers, identify an area you need to study in order to discuss with them the truth of Christ and the written Word. Equip yourself by consulting reliable books like *I Don't Have Enough Faith to Be an Atheist* **by Norman Geisler;** *Darwin on Trial* **or** *The Right Questions* **by Phillip Johnson;** *Reasonable Faith* **by William Craig; and** *The Case for Christ, The Case for the Creator,* **and** *The Case for Faith* **by Lee Strobel.**

Tomorrow we'll study other kinds of doubtful wanderers you might encounter.

DAY 2
MORE DOUBTERS

This week we're studying Thomas, the doubtful wanderer. Before continuing with his story, we stopped to identify different types of doubters, and in day 1 we looked at the empirical doubter. Today we'll look at three more types of doubters: the disillusioned doubter, the disappointed doubter, and the moral doubter.

THE DISILLUSIONED DOUBTER

This kind of doubter says, "Believing would require conclusions I don't see. I just can't make God fit with the world around me." Many have struggled with apparent paradoxes. If God is real, why is the world so messed up? If God is in charge, why do abuse, murder, rape, and abortion plague society? If God cares, why are famine, disease, and natural disaster rampant around the globe? If God is good, why is there suffering in the world?

To address these kinds of doubts, let's first think about the kind of world God decided to make. He wanted a place where people were free to choose. He wanted to create people who were able to make choices.

I've heard people suggest, "Why doesn't God just show us who He is in all His majesty, and then we'd all fall on our faces and worship Him?" But that wouldn't be worship; it would be coercion. God prefers the sincere worship of those who choose Him rather than the robotic worship of the masses.

> **What's your response to the previous sentence?**

> **What are some consequences for a world in which people are free to choose?**

Second Chronicles 15:2 says:

> *The LORD is with you while you are with him.*
> *If you seek him, he will be found by you.*
> **2 CHRONICLES 15:2**

God wants to be found. He wants to be known, believed in, and trusted. He appeals to us in many compelling ways, but He won't coerce us. He's given us a choice.

Could God make a world in which people are free to choose—truly free to decide—and, at the same time, guarantee that everyone would choose Him? No, He couldn't. All the pain, all the heartache, and all the suffering in this world are the results of people not choosing God. The original sin of man, confirmed by every person in every generation since, has left the world in shambles. But like our first ancestors, we desperately want to find someone else to blame for what our choices produce.

At this point skeptics often ask, "What about natural disasters? Whose fault are they?" Isn't it interesting how adamant people can be about blaming God for anything they see as bad, while refusing to give Him credit for the fire hose of blessings that He allows in their lives? A thousand idyllic sunsets on the beach are taken for granted, but a tsunami instantly provokes wrath against God. After a devastating mix of natural, personal, and direct human disasters, Job asked a question we need to ask more often: "Shall we receive good from God, and shall we not receive evil?" (Job 2:10).

Job realized living in a fallen world means experiencing just how messed up creation is because of sin. Paul described it this way:

> *The whole creation has been groaning together*
> *as in the pains of childbirth.*
> **ROMANS 8:22**

The world is broken because of sin. This whole thing is winding down in a hurry. Jesus pointed out that God "sends the rain on the just and on the unjust" (Matt. 5:45).

Just the fact that we get life, breath, and another day in this beautiful universe, as well as a chance to choose the One who made us, should soften our hearts toward Him. He's calling out to us in every moment of every day, "I'm here! I'm real! I love you!" He reached out in His Son, Jesus Christ, and provided the payment for our sins so that we could be reconciled to a holy God. Why aren't we overwhelmed by *those* acts of God? The Bible says God's goodness should lead us to repentance (see Rom. 2:4).

A disillusioned wanderer needs to know that God has done all the real work. All we have to do is realize that He provided salvation, that we need it, and that we must repent of our sin and wandering. We know we've met God when we can't wait to say, "I need Your forgiveness. I believe in You, Lord." He's just asking for a little step of faith, and then He will rush into our lives and transform us. He will cause the Word of God to come alive to us. He will put His Spirit in us and begin to grow and change our hearts and lives. God will do so much if we surrender our disillusionment to the One who holds all the answers.

Have you ever met a disillusioned wanderer who couldn't reconcile God's existence with the state of the world? What hope would you be able to offer today?

THE DISAPPOINTED DOUBTER

Many people are deeply distressed to discover we must come to God on His terms, not on ours. Disappointed doubters often admit that believing would require forgiveness they don't desire to give: "To believe in God, I'll have to settle some things I don't want to settle." Disappointed doubters are bitter. Something deeply hurtful happened to them, and now they're angry, desiring revenge—payback. If you're a disappointed doubter, you want to see others suffer the way they made you suffer. Until that happens, you aren't interested in God.

Unsettled offenses keep a lot of people away from God. Doubt, fueled by angry disappointment, can be a hard challenge to a person's faith. If you've been attacked or betrayed, how do you let that go, move forward, and keep being faithful? It's very hard not to revel in someone's misfortune when that person has caused us pain. It goes against our nature to rejoice when God blesses them.

Here's how God gets in the middle of our hunger for fairness. To embrace God with my whole heart, I've got to come to grips with the fact that He allowed something awful to happen in my life. I've got to forgive that person. I've got to embrace God's will for me as having a good purpose even though I can't see it or imagine it.

Do you know any disappointed doubters? What bitterness are they holding on to?

Read the following verses and record solutions to the problem of bitterness toward others.

Matthew 5:11

Matthew 5:44

Romans 12:14

Forgiveness displaces the spiritual barrier in a disappointed doubter. Forgiveness is the decision to release a person from the obligation that resulted when he or she injured you.

Sometimes people sink into doubt and reject God's forgiveness because believing would require them to forgive someone else. Jesus' parable of the unforgiving servant teaches that we can't have forgiveness if we're not willing to pass it on to others (see Matt. 18:23-35). That's how disillusioned people wipe out and start wandering. A disappointed doubter's pathway home comes through forgiveness—their own and others'.

THE MORAL DOUBTER

Moral doubters make their case in the following manner: "To embrace God by faith with my whole heart, I'd have to make some changes I frankly don't want to make." Instead, moral doubters perpetuate the condition of uncertainty to avoid the implications of acknowledging a Supreme Being. Among these are:

- If God is supreme, then I'm not a free moral agent.

- If God is supreme, then I must live the way my Creator requires.

- If God is supreme, then I can't do what I want with impunity.

Romans 1:18 tells us that moral doubters "by their unrighteousness suppress the truth." They know what they're doing, but they don't realize what it's costing them—peace with God now and eternity with Him later.

What kinds of things would moral doubters have to give up in order to surrender their lives to God?

Do you remember the jack-in-the-boxes we used to have when we were kids? You'd spin the handle and hear the familiar tune. Then you braced yourself for the flap to spring, and "Pop goes the weasel!"

I think God is like that in many people's lives. As the music of life plays out, pop! God shows up. Push down the flap—there, God is gone. Maybe He was just your imagination. The music goes on—pop! And there's God again. The problem with willfully doubting God's appearances is that you're really revealing an attitude: "I don't want to answer to Him. I don't want to explain what I'm doing." But you can't get away from Him. In one way or another, He will continue to show up.

David asked:

> *Where shall I go from your Spirit?*
> *Or where shall I flee from your presence?*
> **PSALM 139:7**

David had to admit there was nowhere to escape from God.

Doubter of every kind, let go of doubt instead of holding on to it as if it can explain your life or give you direction. Find in the Lord all you've been longing for. He's been pursuing you every step of your wandering.

Pray for any empirical, disillusioned, disappointed, or moral doubters you know. Ask God to show you ways you can reach out to them and guide them back to the truth.

DAY 3

HOW GOD DEALS WITH DOUBTERS

Today we'll go back to Thomas, the world's most famous doubter, to find out how God deals with doubtful wanderers.

DOUBTING THOMAS

John 20:24 begins, **"Thomas, one of the Twelve, called the Twin ..."** The Greek for *Twin* is *Didymus*. The first time Thomas is referenced as "the Twin" is in John 11:16. This verse gives us a very different perspective on Thomas, for in this account Thomas isn't a passive doubter at all. I'm sticking up for him here, on behalf of the doubters in our midst. Thomas wasn't some lame guy who was proud of his doubts.

In John 11 Jesus announced He was going to Bethany to raise Lazarus, even though it was apparent the Jewish leaders in Jerusalem were plotting to kill Him. The disciples didn't like the idea that Jesus was placing Himself in danger. But it was Thomas who spoke up:

> *Thomas, called the Twin, said to his fellow disciples,*
> *"Let us also go, that we may die with Him."*
> **JOHN 11:16**

This guy was committed to the Lord, but he had doubts—along with a good dose of pessimism.

Later, in John 14 we find these words spoken by Jesus:

> *Let not your hearts be troubled. Believe in God; believe*
> *also in me. ... I go to prepare a place for you.*
> **JOHN 14:1-3**

Thomas then asked Jesus:

"Lord, we do not know where you are going. How can we know the way?" Jesus said to him, "I am the way. ... No one comes to the Father except through me."
JOHN 14:5-6

Thomas is so straight-up. I love people like him. He was saying, "I have a question! I don't get it!" He was honest enough to admit his questions and doubts and to articulate them.

Why is it important to admit any spiritual doubts we may have?

When Jesus died, Thomas must have been devastated. At that point Thomas may have been a disillusioned doubter or a disappointed doubter. When Jesus first appeared to the disciples as a group on resurrection day, Thomas wasn't present:

On the evening of that day, the first day of the week, the doors being locked where the disciples were for fear of the Jews, Jesus came and stood among them and said to them, "Peace be with you." When he had said this, he showed them his hands and his side. Then the disciples were glad when they saw the Lord.
JOHN 20:19-20

If Thomas had been with the rest of the disciples on resurrection day, he would have seen Jesus. His doubts would have vanished. His faith would have soared.

Describe a time when a fresh encounter with Jesus allayed any doubts or wandering in your walk with Him.

THE ANTIDOTE TO DOUBT

So far this week we've studied a lot about different types of doubters. It's important to understand that doubt doesn't disappear on its own. Jesus didn't simply vaporize Thomas's doubt. Doubt has to be replaced with something. And that something is faith.

Throughout the life of Jesus we see Him calling people out of their doubts into a life of faith in Him. In Matthew 14 Peter attempted to walk on the water, but his courage faltered when he saw the waves, and he began to sink. Jesus rescued Him, saying, "O you of little faith, why did you doubt?" (v. 31).

Jesus commended expressions of faith that He encountered, such as the faith of the Centurion (see Matt. 8:10), the woman with the discharge of blood (see Matt. 9:22), and the men who brought their paralytic friend to be healed by Jesus (see Mark 2:5).

I've discovered five truths about the way faith overcomes doubt.

FAITH IS DEAD WHEN THE HEART IS PASSIVE. Doubt flourishes when the heart isn't engaged. Many people have passive hearts. They're not actively seeking God.

You may think, *Oh, I wish I were one of those people who have deep faith. I'm just not one of those faith people.* The problem is, you aren't doing what faith people do in order to have more faith. You're just like a person who's in the middle of a room watching everything that's happening, but you're not part of it. Being a spectator of life isn't really living; watching faith in action isn't practicing faith.

> **Have you ever had a passive heart toward God? How does a passive heart create spiritual doubts?**

Complaining about persistent doubts—if you're never in the place where faith is built— is like complaining about the darkness in your basement under a blanket with the lights off. If you want faith, you've got to get to the places where faith flourishes. Let me give you some places where faith flourishes.

- *Faith flourishes in the Word of God.* Romans 10:17 tells us, "Faith comes from hearing … the word of Christ." That's why we go to church: to hear the Word of God. Our faith is lifted by exposure to God's Word. Strengthened faith is a by-product of Word-informed, Christ-centered worship.

- *Faith flourishes with the people of God.* Friendship with people of faith increases our faith. If you don't have relationships with people of faith, you're undermining your faith. When you're surrounded by doubters, doubting comes easily.

Are you in a small group? Are you intentionally connected with other people of faith? Are you fellowshipping with Christians? When you have an evening to spare, whom do you associate with? What do you talk about?

What are your responses to those questions?

Hebrews 10:24 says, "Let us consider how to stir up one another to love and good works." Being with the people of God should stir faith within you.

- *Faith flourishes in the household of God.* Going to church is a continual exercise in strengthening faith. Faith flourishes when you gather around the Word of God with a group of believers. Go to church. Go every week. Don't just make it a habit; make it your lifestyle. Go meet Him and have your faith charged up.

How has church involvement strengthened your faith?

Hebrews 10:25 says:

> ... *not neglecting to meet together, as is the habit of some,*
> *but encouraging one another.*
> **HEBREWS 10:25**

So Thomas wasn't with the other disciples when Jesus first appeared to them. He wasn't where he needed to be for faith to flourish:

> *Thomas, one of the Twelve ... was not with them when Jesus came.*
> *So the other disciples told him, "We have seen the Lord."*
> **JOHN 20:24-25**

Actually, the Greek verb tense means "They kept on saying, 'We've seen the Lord.'" It's kind of hard to be a Thomas. You know what it's like when you've missed the memo. The other disciples kept saying, "We saw the Lord! We saw the Lord!"

Thomas's answer may strike us as odd, but we'll find out it wasn't prideful:

Unless I see in His hands the mark of the nails, and place my finger into the mark of the nails, and place my hand into His side, I will never believe.
JOHN 20:25

Some people have considered Thomas's words demanding and disrespectful. But we've already seen that Thomas wasn't with his fellow disciples at Jesus' first appearance. If he had been, he would have seen Jesus' hands and side. Thomas was only asking for what he'd missed. He was expressing a willingness to believe, based on the same evidence given to the people around him. His request wasn't unreasonable. He didn't want to doubt; he wanted to believe. Thomas's heart wasn't passive. He was on his way to faith.

How have past spiritual doubts led you to greater faith?

FAITH IS KINDLED WHEN THE HEART IDENTIFIES THE OBSTACLE. Thomas was sincere. He wanted to believe. He wanted a faith on fire. Now he'd named the obstacle. Faith is kindled when you name the obstacle.

Name the obstacle to faith in your life: "I got hurt. I have a question I don't have an answer for. I'm discouraged. I don't honestly understand how Christianity can be true." Name the obstacle: "Lord, this is the barrier between You and me."

I've often heard people say, "I finally became open to faith when I admitted my life was empty and out of control." The moment you name the obstacle, faith is going to start growing in you. It's counterintuitive but true. If you're a doubter, I challenge you to name the obstacle. Produce the reasons you're doubting and give God an opportunity to replace doubt with faith.

Have you admitted any doubt that currently exists in your heart? If not, confess it and talk to the Lord about it now. Ask Him to replace it with faith.

Tomorrow we'll continue with additional ways faith is kindled to replace the nagging doubts in our lives.

DAY 4
FAITH ON FIRE

Yesterday we started examining faith as the antidote to doubt. We deal with doubt by replacing it with faith. We mentioned that faith is dead when the heart is passive, and faith is kindled when the heart identifies the obstacle. Today we'll look at three more truths about the way faith grows in our lives.

FAITH IS SPARKED WHEN THE LORD REVEALS HIMSELF AT OUR POINT OF NEED. When we see God at work amid our doubts, faith is sparked. Thomas had named the obstacle—his doubt that Jesus had been resurrected—and now the Lord would reveal Himself. As He did with Peter, Jesus answered in His timing. Thomas had to wait:

> *Eight days later, his disciples were inside again, and Thomas was with them. Although the doors were locked, Jesus came and stood among them and said, "Peace be with you."*
> **JOHN 20:26**

Notice the precision involved in what Jesus said next:

> *He said to Thomas, "Put your finger here, and see my hands; and put out your hand, and place it in my side."*
> **JOHN 20:27**

Those were the exact words Thomas had used in expressing his doubt. Did Jesus understand Thomas's obstacle? He did. And He answered in a way that settled things in Thomas's heart.

> **How has God revealed Himself to you in times of doubts?**

FAITH IS IGNITED WHEN THE HEART SUBMITS TO THE REVELATION. Thomas submitted to the revelation God arranged. Jesus told him, **"Do not disbelieve, but believe" (v. 27)**, implying he had a choice. Thomas answered, **"My Lord and my God!" (v. 28)**. Isn't that response awesome? One moment Thomas was thinking, *I don't get it.*

I don't see it. Then Jesus showed up, and the doubter immediately said, "I get it! I see it! This is my Lord and my God!" Thomas's faith was ignited.

Thomas's expression "my Lord" meant *my rightful Ruler, my Master, my Sovereign, King of my life*. He was pulling out all the stops on submission. Then he added "my God," meaning *beyond me, above me, uniquely different from me, and worthy of my worship and adoration*. "My Lord and my God!" beautifully expresses Thomas's complete surrender to Christ. Now his faith was on fire.

If you're a doubter, a moment like Thomas's is what it's going to take to break your pattern of doubt. You've got to submit to the revelation God brings into your life. Wait for God to make Himself known. Then respond as Thomas did to God's presence in your life.

The Lord will go a long way in revealing Himself to an honest, sincere Thomas. You might wonder, *What would've happened if Jesus had shown up, scars and all, and then Thomas had answered, "Nah, I still don't believe"*? I've never seen that kind of rejection happen. Doubt is dispersed when someone meets the risen Christ.

Read Mark 9:17-27. How would you describe the faith of the boy's father?

Like this father, Thomas had the "want to" of faith. And his faith was set on fire. If you have no sincere interest in growing in faith, you'll remain as you are.

FAITH IS ABLAZE WHEN IT COMES BEFORE SEEING. Practicing a mature faith is the way we want to live our lives. That's what Jesus exhorted when He said in His response to Thomas:

> *Have you believed because you have seen me? Blessed are those who have not seen and yet have believed.*
> **JOHN 20:29**

The writer of Hebrews reminds us:

> *Without faith it is impossible to please him, for whoever would draw near to God must believe that he exists and that he rewards those who seek him.*
> **HEBREWS 11:6**

We want to get to the place where we don't have to see to believe. We want to grow into followers of Jesus who can say, "I trust Him. He's right. He's true. I don't have to keep asking God to reconfirm what He's shown me."

Many of the people who came to Jesus for healing displayed that kind of faith. They'd seen Jesus at work, and by approaching Him with their need, they submitted to His revelation of His power. That gave them faith to come to Him and ask for healing. Jesus affirmed these people who acted on their faith.

Identify a time when you acted on faith without being able to see the outcome.

God delights to hear His children say, "It's enough! I believe every word You say. I trust everything You tell me. I'm not going to put my questions ahead of obedience; I'm going to obey and let You settle any questions in Your time. You're God, and I'm not—and I like it that way."

When you get to that place, the doubtful wanderer you once were will be a memory in your rearview mirror. You'll be looking forward to where God is taking you, excited to be traveling under His direction, knowing all the while that you're actually home.

Answer the following questions about your doubts.

Is your heart passive?

Have you identified the obstacle to belief?

Has God revealed Himself at the point of your need?

Has your heart submitted to God's revelation of Himself?

Do you have faith even before seeing God's answer?

Pray about your responses and ask God to take you to the next level of faith by giving you a heart that wants to know Him.

DAY 5

BRINGING THE WANDERER HOME

Doubting is common in the lives of many believers. If we've been through times of doubt, God can use us to demonstrate abundant grace to wanderers who doubt.

> **Look back in week 1, day 5 at your list of the wanderers in your life. Identify any who fit the description of a doubtful wanderer. Keep them in mind as you complete today's lesson.**

THE EMPIRICAL DOUBTER

Empirical doubters have trouble with God's logic. They may doubt God's existence, creation, miracles, Jesus' resurrection, or the Bible. Often these doubters are honestly having trouble reconciling what they've heard with what's true. Other times an empirical doubter may be looking for an excuse to avoid faith.

> **Should we treat the honest doubter differently from someone who's avoiding faith? Why or why not?**

> **How would you answer someone doubting God's existence?**

> **Doubting creation?**

> **Doubting miracles?**

Doubting Jesus' resurrection?

Doubting the reliability of the Bible?

THE DISILLUSIONED DOUBTER

Disillusioned doubters have trouble reconciling what they've heard about God with what they know about the world. It's difficult for any human to see the pain and destruction in the world and understand that God is good. It's difficult, even impossible, to fully reconcile human free will with God's sovereignty.

> **When have you encountered a disillusioned doubter? How did you answer his concerns?**

Many times disillusioned doubts center on a specific circumstance in the doubter's life. Often this is a time of pain for the doubter. So when we go get these doubters, we must be gentle, remembering not only truth but also grace.

> **How can you use your own story to demonstrate God's goodness in the midst of hardship and pain?**

> **What are ways we can demonstrate God's love while acknowledging the truth about His sovereignty?**

THE DISAPPOINTED DOUBTER

Disappointed doubters are difficult to go and bring home. They're often angry, bitter, and frustrated with God and His people. They're in pain and not yet ready to forgive those who may have hurt them.

How can you show love to a wanderer who's angry, bitter, and unforgiving?

How can you demonstrate the peace and forgiveness God calls them to?

THE MORAL DOUBTER

Moral doubters are afraid they'll have to change their way of life if they go back home. They think the life they have wandering is more fun and fulfilling than the life they'd have in Christ. We know this isn't true. A wanderer's life may provide temporary pleasures, but it won't bring lasting joy.

When going to get a moral doubter, we must keep in mind that because we're all sinners, we were God's enemies when Jesus died for us (see Rom. 5:6-8). Therefore, we must show grace and forgiveness to a moral doubter.

How can you demonstrate grace while persuading a moral doubter of the truth?

How do your life and your words prove that God's way is best?

HELPING WANDERERS CULTIVATE FAITH

The opposite of doubt is faith. If doubting wanderers are to come home, they'll need to come to a place where they have faith in God. It's impossible to force other people to have faith, but there are some things we can do to help cultivate a wanderer's faith.

Identify a time when you had faith before seeing the result God was going to bring about. How can you share that experience with a doubtful wanderer?

Faith flourishes in the Word of God, with the people of God, and in the household of God. Most doubters have gone without one or all of these supports for some time.

What are some ways you can teach and display God's Word to a doubting wanderer in your life?

Read Hebrews 10:24-25. How can you "stir up" (v. 24), or encourage, a doubter in your life?

Many times doubters no longer attend church. What are some ways you can help them be open to the household of God?

In the passages we studied this week, we saw Thomas name his obstacle to faith. In turn, Jesus demonstrated grace and patience in addressing Thomas's doubt.

How can you help others identify their obstacles to faith?

How can you demonstrate grace and patience as you go get doubtful wanderers?

PRAY FOR THE DOUBTFUL WANDERER

Pray that God will turn the hearts of doubtful wanderers back to Him. Pray that they'll be satisfied with the truth found in His Word. Pray that the doubtful wanderer's heart and eyes will be opened to the peace of faith. Pray that God will show you ways to demonstrate patience, grace, and love for the doubtful wanderers in your life.

SENSUAL WANDERER, COME HOME

START

**WELCOME BACK TO THIS GROUP
DISCUSSION OF** *COME HOME.*

The previous group session's application activity involved noting times
when you doubted God's character or promises, the circumstances
giving rise to that doubt, and times when you were less likely to doubt.
If you're comfortable, share your experiences from the past week.

Describe what you liked best about the lessons in week 3.
What questions do you have?

How can you encourage faith in the wanderers you know as you
interact with them?

Today's study will focus on the sensual wanderer. What comes to mind
when you hear the word *sensual?*

To prepare for the DVD segment, read aloud the following verses.

> *When Delilah saw that he [Samson] had told her
> all his heart, she sent and called the lords of the
> Philistines, saying, "Come up again, for he has told
> me all his heart." Then the lords of the Philistines
> came up to her and brought the money in their
> hands. She made him sleep on her knees. And she
> called a man and had him shave off the seven locks
> of his head. Then she began to torment him, and his
> strength left him. And she said, "The Philistines are
> upon you, Samson!" And he awoke from his sleep
> and said, "I will go out as at other times and shake
> myself free." But he did not know that the L*ORD* had
> left him. And the Philistines seized him and gouged
> out his eyes and brought him down to Gaza and
> bound him with bronze shackles. And he ground
> at the mill in the prison.*
> **JUDGES 16:18-21**

WATCH

Sensual: pertaining to, inclined to, or preoccupied with the gratification of my _____

A sensual person is consumed with indulging their own _____.

I want _____ to be the only influence that reigns supreme in my life.

As long as any desire for anything is reigning in my life, I'm not controlled by God, and I am a _____ person.

Incomplete obedience equals ongoing _____.

Sensual wanderers have no _____.

For the sensual wanderer, people are always _____.

Sensual wanderers are controlled by _____.

Sensual wanderers are oblivious to the _____.

Sensual wandering ruins _____.

Sensual wanderers are getting worse and growing _____.

Sensual wanderers will be _____ by God Himself.

It's not the suppression of desire. It's directing desire toward that which truly _____.

It's not too late for sensual wanderers to _____ _____.

DISCUSS THE DVD SEGMENT WITH YOUR GROUP, USING THE QUESTIONS BELOW.

What's something new you learned from James's teaching about Samson, the sensual wanderer?

What are some forms of sensual wandering?

Why is sensual wandering a strong temptation for believers today?

How does a sensual lifestyle cause someone to disrespect God and others?

Read 1 Corinthians 6:12. How does sensual indulgence lead to enslavement? What forms of enslavement do you see in the lives of sensual wanderers you know?

Why are sensual wanderers oblivious to the carnage they're causing?

Discuss James's statement that the solution to sensuality isn't "the suppression of desire. It's directing desire toward that which truly satisfies."

Is it ever too late for a sensual wanderer to repent and come home? Why or why not?

Application. This week make notes of ways our culture promotes unbridled sensuality. Be prepared to share during the next group session.

This week's Scripture memory.

"All things are lawful for me," but not all things are helpful. "All things are lawful for me," but I will not be enslaved by anything.
1 CORINTHIANS 6:12

Assignment. Read week 4 and complete the activities before the next group experience. Consider going deeper into this content by reading chapter 4 in James MacDonald's book *Come Home* (Moody Publishers, 2013).

SENSUAL WANDERER, COME HOME

In 2014 the governor of Vermont surprised everyone by devoting his entire state-of-the-state address to the problem of heroin abuse. He quoted the shocking statistic that heroin abuse had increased 770 percent in Vermont since 2000.

Vermont's problem is just the tip of the iceberg. Heroin abuse among first-time users in the United States has increased by almost 60 percent in the past decade. Facing increased costs and regulations in obtaining nonmedical prescription painkillers, drug users have turned to heroin because it's cheaper and easier to buy.[1] The consequence has been a rapidly growing number of deaths from drug overdoses.

Heroin addiction is just one in a long list of social ills that have resulted from America's obsession with sensual pleasures. Nobody sets out to destroy their lives. But one thing leads to another, and whether through alcohol, drugs, or sexual immorality, the result is a painful story of addiction, wrecked relationships, and wasted potential.

The Bible issues ample warnings about the dangers of sensual living and presents the stories of several people whose lives veered off course and crashed. Samson was one of those sensual wanderers. His tragic example can make us sensitive to the sensual wanderers in our lives and can encourage us to get them back on course before it's too late.

1. David DiSalvo, "Why Is Heroin Abuse Rising While Other Drug Abuse Is Falling?" *Forbes* [online], 14 January 2014 [cited 21 March 2014]. Available from the *Internet: www.forbes.com*.

DAY 1
THE SENSUAL WANDERER

So far we've studied the fearful wanderer, Peter, and the doubtful wanderer, Thomas. I hope you've been able to identify people in your life who are wandering from God, as well as your own tendencies to wander from the truth. Our study's based on this important admonition from the Book of James:

> My brothers, if anyone among you wanders from the truth and someone brings him back, let him know that whoever brings back a sinner from his wandering will save his soul from death and will cover a multitude of sins.
> **JAMES 5:19-20**

The next wanderer we'll examine is the sensual wanderer, and I think you'll readily recognize this type of wanderer among the people you know.

What comes to your mind when you see or hear the word *sensual*?

CONSUMED WITH SELF-INDULGENCE

Let's begin with a good definition of the word *sensual*. Many people equate that term with sexual activity. This reflects a frequent misunderstanding of the word. The term *sensual* includes, but isn't limited to, sexual activity. Sensual can be sexual, but the term also encompasses many other expressions of sensuality that lead to wandering from God. The word actually means *pertaining to, inclined to, or preoccupied with the gratification of the body*. The idea comes from a Latin word, *sensualis,* which means *of the senses; the pursuit of that which pleases the senses*. Sensual people, then, are consumed with indulging their own desires. Let's look at some areas of sensual desire that people struggle with.

FOOD. An obsession with food is common in our culture. Food stirs a desire that isn't wrong in itself—hunger—but can become wrong and unhealthy. Figures from the Centers for Disease Control indicate more than a third of the population of the United States falls into the obese category.[1] The craving for food can be a sensual problem.

ENTERTAINMENT. Entertainment is a huge form of sensuality in our culture. Americans annually spend billions of dollars to rent and download movies and television shows.[2] In addition, the average person watches more than five hours of television each day.[3] One in eight Americans has an Internet addiction.[4]

LEGAL SUBSTANCES. Legal substances are another category that attracts and exhausts people's senses. For example, four hundred billion cups of coffee are consumed every year,[5] making caffeine the most commonly taken mind-altering substance on the planet.[6] A more serious legal substance is alcohol. Addiction to alcohol is shredding the fabric of our society. There isn't a social evil that isn't significantly amplified by alcohol. Alcohol takes everything wrong in our hearts and turns up the volume on all of it while drowning out the attempts of conscience to urge caution. Alcohol scrambles our senses.

ILLEGAL SUBSTANCES. Statistics show that more than 20 million people in the United States use illegal drugs. Marijuana is the most common, psychotherapeutics are second, and cocaine is third. Drug use among high-school students is going down slightly, but it increased by 50 percent among people over 50 years of age during the past few years.[7] Ironically, people desire illegal drugs not to pursue heightened senses but to numb the pain of life.

IMMORALITY. Sexual sin is what we often equate with sensuality. Christianity teaches that sex is a good gift created by God and intended for pleasure and procreation within marriage. But outside the lines God has prescribed, sex can be wrongly used for evil. According to the Guttmacher Institute, by the age of 19 over half of men and women have had intercourse.[8]

The definition of *deviance* is being watered down in our society so that fewer and fewer people consider any behavior sexually abnormal or perverse. An increasing percentage of Americans believe that cohabitation, adultery, homosexuality, and pornography are morally acceptable behaviors. What was hidden and shameful has become promoted and in some cases protected by the weight of law. What the Bible calls sin, the world accepts as personal rights not to be infringed on or even questioned by anyone.

Think about people you know who've wandered from God because of sensual sins. Record the effects of those sins in their lives.

If we don't indulge in any of the sensual sins I've just mentioned, we can't be smug and self-satisfied. We probably deal with other sensual temptations that threaten to drive a wedge between us and God. The apostle Paul commonly warned his readers about a variety of vices—sensual sins—that aren't compatible with Christian living.

> Read Ephesians 5:3-4 and Colossians 3:5-9. What sensual sins did Paul identify?

> Read 1 Corinthians 6:12. How do Christians know whether a sensual pleasure has too much sway in their lives?

As Christians, we want God to be the *only* influence that reigns supreme in our lives. If any sensual desire or activity rules us, we aren't controlled by God. We're behaving as sensually minded people. This week's study is for every humble person who wants more of the good things God offers and less of the sinful things that consume us but never really deliver what they promise.

SAMSON, THE SENSUAL

People often know fragments about the Old Testament figure named Samson: long hair, great strength, Delilah. They may not realize that Samson was a sensual person. Judges 13 introduces Samson through his parents, who were barren but were given a miracle child. An angel suddenly appeared and announced to Samson's parents:

> *You shall conceive and bear a son. No razor shall come upon his head, for the child shall be a Nazirite to God from the womb, and he shall begin to save Israel from the hand of the Philistines.*
> **JUDGES 13:5**

Samson was raised as a Nazirite. In the Old Testament a Nazirite was a person who took a vow to belong totally to God. Today Christians say we belong totally to God; that's what the lordship of Jesus Christ is all about. But in Old Testament days the culture specified certain behavior to indicate God's ownership. A Nazirite vow meant the following.

1. The person abstained from all wine and strong drink. It's always interesting to me how often the Bible reports that people who belong totally to God, whether they were priests or Nazirites, stayed away from alcohol.

2. Nazirites were forbidden to touch a corpse, whether a person or an animal.

3. Nazirites weren't allowed to cut their hair for the duration of the vow, which in Samson's case was a lifetime.

These signs were intended to remind the person of God's ownership. He was to be prompted by these practical, everyday choices to remember, *My life belongs totally to God.* As we look at the life of Samson, we'll see that sadly, pathetically, his life didn't belong to God; it belonged to Samson. He was a sensual person. Though he grew up under God's blessing, his attention was drawn to pleasure like a moth to a bug zapper. It was only a matter of time before he wandered from God.

Maybe you know sensual wanderers whose lives are spinning out of control because they're addicted to drugs or caught up in entertainment and pleasure, with no sense of priorities and no room for God. It's time for those wanderers to come home.

> **Start praying for sensual wanderers you know to see the futility of their indulgence and come home. Pray that God will use you to bring them back.**

Even if you don't struggle with strong sensual temptations as Samson did, this week's study will provide a good opportunity for you to examine your commitment to Christ. Just as a Nazirite was supposed to be totally devoted to serving God, so is every Christian today. If your heart completely belongs to Him, you won't indulge traces of sensuality that could reign over your life, causing you to miss the purpose God has planned for you.

> **Pray about any sensual indulgences that have too strong a hold in your own life, that God will help you recognize these and begin to break these habits as you put Him first in your life.**

1. "Adult Obesity Facts," *Centers for Disease Control and Prevention* [online], 16 August 2013 [cited 28 March 2014]. Available from the Internet: *www.cdc.gov.*
2. "Unkind Rewind," *The Economist* [online], 17 March 2011 [cited 28 March 2014]. Available from the Internet: *www.economist.com.*
3. David Hinckley, "Average American Watches Five Hours of TV per Day, Report Shows," *New York Daily News* [online], 5 March 2014 [cited 28 March 2014]. Available from the Internet: *www.nydailynews.com.*
4. Kimberly Young, *Net Addiction* [online, cited 28 March 2014]. Available from the Internet: *www.netaddiction.com.*
5. "Where Starbucks Went Wrong," *WorldHealth.net* [online], 29 July 2008 [cited 28 March 2014]. Available from the Internet: *www.worldhealth.net.*
6. "Caffeine Facts," *Australian Drug Foundation* [online], 13 January 2013 [cited 28 March 2014]. Available from the Internet: *www.druginfo.adf.org.au.*
7. "Drug Facts: Nationwide Trends," *National Institute on Drug Abuse* [online], January 2014 [cited 28 March 2014]. Available from the Internet: *www.drugabuse.gov.*
8. "Facts on American Teens' Sexual and Reproductive Health," *Guttmacher Institute* [online], June 2013 [cited 28 March 2014]. Available from the Internet: *www.guttmacher.org.*

DAY 2
OUT OF CONTROL

Yesterday we were introduced to Samson, and today we'll discover why he's the poster child for sensual indulgence. Immediately in Judges 14 we begin to see in Samson the profile of a sensual wanderer:

> *Samson went down to Timnah, and at Timnah*
> *he saw one of the daughters of the Philistines.*
> **JUDGES 14:1**

To understand Samson's story, we need some historical background. The Philistines were the archenemies of the nation of Israel. The Philistines were among the people God had instructed Joshua and Israel to remove from the promised land. They weren't supposed to be around. God gave Joshua the authority and the armies to expel them. But the Israelites thought, *Why clear the land of our enemies? We've got our space here. Everything's good. Let's all coexist.* Because they didn't finish the job God had given them, they lived with ongoing problems with the Philistines for generations. Incomplete obedience invites ongoing problems.

The angel who announced Samson's birth had indicated the purpose God had for Samson: **"He shall begin to save Israel from the hand of the Philistines"** (Judg. 13:5).

The Philistines were an enemy, a deadly nuisance. God raised Samson and gave him special strength to drive the Philistines out. But instead of using his abilities to do the job God assigned him, he wanted to satisfy his sensual self. His failure set the stage for later disasters, like the capture of the ark of the covenant and the contest between David and Goliath. Those confrontations involved the Philistines. We can see the pattern today. Again, incomplete obedience invites ongoing problems.

> **Describe a time in your life when incomplete obedience created problems down the road.**

We see signs that Samson was becoming a sensual wanderer when he chose to interact with the enemy. He came back from Timnah with a Philistine girl on his mind:

> He came up and told his father and mother, "I saw
> one of the daughters of the Philistines at Timnah."
> **JUDGES 14:2**

Now *saw* here doesn't mean *observed*. Samson wasn't saying, "Oh, I noticed this girl." He saw her. His senses redlined. He was smitten.

Even after he saw her, he could have walked away. Instead, he plunged into wandering when he told his parents, **"Get her for me as my wife" (v. 2)**. At this point in the story we start to notice troubling characteristics of a sensual wanderer, as demonstrated in the life of Samson.

SENSUAL WANDERERS HAVE NO RESPECT

Despite his remarkable upbringing, Samson displayed a stunning lack of respect. The word *respect* means *to esteem, to show deference to a person of value who's worthy of honor*. Because of his sensual leanings, Samson developed no proper respect.

SAMSON HAD NO RESPECT FOR GOD'S LAW. God's law forbade marriage outside the people of Israel (see Lev. 21:14), but Samson wanted this Philistine woman as his wife.

SAMSON HAD NO RESPECT FOR GOD'S CALLING. He never stopped to think that God had given him his great strength for a divine purpose. He knew the Philistine woman was forbidden, but he wanted what was forbidden, and nothing was going to stop him. He was a sensual person.

SAMSON HAD NO RESPECT FOR HIS PARENTS. When he told them to get the Philistine woman to be his wife, they responded:

> Is there not a woman among the daughters of your relatives,
> or among all our people, that you must go to take a wife from
> the uncircumcised Philistines?
> **JUDGES 14:3**

But their feelings and objections meant nothing to Samson. He replied, **"Get her for me, for she is right in my eyes" (v. 3)**. Samson callously cast his parents aside to please himself.

SAMSON HAD NO RESPECT FOR HIMSELF. Samson was a man called and gifted by God. He had an incredible opportunity to bless others. Instead, his goal became to satisfy his sensual self, and nothing was going to get in his way.

Samson had no respect. Or to be technically correct, he had a sensually distorted respect. He *did* show deference to his own desires. He exercised esteem and gave honor to his sensual self at the expense of his true self. Sensual wanderers exhibit a lack of respect.

> **Read about another sensual wanderer in 2 Samuel 11:1-5. How did David show disrespect for God and others?**

> **Identify a time when your desire overruled your respect for others, yourself, or God.**

SENSUAL WANDERERS ARE CONTROLLED BY THEIR APPETITES

Although Samson had remarkable capabilities, he allowed himself to be controlled by his appetites. Like the lives of all sensual wanderers, Samson's life was out of control. Judges 14:8 reports, **"After some days he returned to take her."** Notice Samson didn't return to woo her or to win the woman's affections; he didn't ask or invite. For the sensual wanderer, people are always things to be used. People are props in the sensual wanderer's personal drama.

We don't always realize how often, and in what different forms, self-centeredness shows up in our lives. The sensual wanderer hears only one voice—appetite: "I want what I want. I need this to feed my sensual self."

Judges 14 continues:

> *He [Samson] turned aside to see the carcass of the lion, and behold, there was a swarm of bees in the body of the lion, and honey.*
> **JUDGES 14:8**

As a Nazirite, Samson knew he wasn't allowed to touch dead things. But that didn't matter to him. He was hungry! He needed a sugar fix!

He scraped it out into his hands and went on, eating as he went.
And he came to his father and mother and gave some to them,
and they ate. But he did not tell them that he had scraped the
honey from the carcass of the lion.
JUDGES 14:9

So not only did Samson sin, but he also ceremonially defiled his parents. Why didn't God's law stop Samson? Why didn't he say to himself, *That's wrong. I can't do that?* Because he was a sensual person who had learned never to deny his appetites.

What cravings tempt you to subjugate everything else to what you want?

SENSUAL WANDERERS ARE OBLIVIOUS TO THE CARNAGE

Sensual wanderers are flat-out blind to the impact their choices are making on others. If you've felt the pain of loving a sensual wanderer, you've probably asked yourself, *Don't they see the damage they're doing?* The answer is no. Others are a channel the sensual wanderer never tunes in to. They can't hear, see, or feel beyond their own desires.

The rest of Judges 14 describes Samson's wedding to the Philistine woman. In those times they had a seven-day wedding feast. At the end of the seventh day, the couple consummated the marriage, and then the two were considered married. He'd have called her his wife, but they didn't come together until the end of the seventh day.

During the feast Samson gave the people a riddle:

> *Out of the eater came something to eat.*
> *Out of the strong came something sweet.*
> **JUDGES 14:14**

Then he said, "I'll make you a bet. If you can tell me the answer to that riddle by the last day of the feast, I'll give you 30 pieces of linen and 30 changes of clothing. If you can't tell me, then you've got to give me those items."

They took the bet, but they had a plan. They told Samson's wife to entice Samson to tell them the riddle, or they'd burn her and her father's house (see v. 15). Faced with such a threat, she worked Samson over with weeping, sighing, and comments like "You hate me. You don't love me. Tell me the riddle." For a while Samson held his ground. But she persisted, **"and on the seventh day he told her, because she pressed him hard" (v.17).** Even in this situation, given a choice between integrity under pressure or satisfaction, Samson made the sensual choice. By this point in the story, it's obvious that anyone who understood the chink in Samson's armor could control him.

No sooner had Samson confided in his bride than she passed on the answer to her people (see vv. 17-18). About this time Samson should have said to himself, *This pagan woman is probably never going to be on my team. It's obvious she's going to be here for her family and not for me.* But that's not what he did. Instead, he got furiously angry. He went out and killed 30 men, stripped off their clothes, and delivered them to those who had solved the riddle.

Samson took no lessons away from that disaster. Sensual people are among the hardest to teach because they quickly forget their past mistakes when desire comes knocking. They're oblivious to the carnage they're causing even in their own lives.

> **Have you known sensual wanderers who refused to learn from the consequences of their actions? Give an example.**

Samson was a sensual wanderer, and he let his appetites rule everything in his life and derail his opportunity to be what God wanted him to be. Perhaps Samson's story has reminded you of times in your life when you've ignored God's will and pursued what you wanted, no matter the cost: "I want this, and I want it now." This week's study, though a sad reminder that we have the freedom to live our lives that way, also gives us a chance to stop being a sensual wanderer and come back to the purpose God has for our lives.

> **Take this opportunity to pray and repent of any behaviors that are placing your sensual appetites above God and other people.**

DAY 3

GETTING WORSE AND GROWING WEAKER

Samson wasn't getting off to a good start. God had called him to a great purpose and had given him great strength to accomplish it, but Samson had other ideas. Always ready to give in to his desires, Samson was the quintessential sensual wanderer. Let's see where his sensual wandering was taking him.

SENSUAL WANDERERS ARE GETTING WORSE

Judges 15 continues the story:

> *After some days, at the time of wheat harvest,*
> *Samson went to visit his wife with a young goat.*
> **JUDGES 15:1**

Notice a few days had passed. Sensual wanderers eventually come out of the stupor and return to the mess they've made. They may even regret what the pleasure cost. By going back to this woman, Samson was really saying, "I want my sin, and I want my way." Sensual wanderers always claim rights and expect no consequences. They make statements like "I want my sin *and* my health," "I want my sin *and* my family," "I want my sin *and* my ministry." The bottom line for sensual wanderers doesn't include turning away from sin; it always retains the sin and wants more. They admit, "When push comes to shove between pleasure and good, I'm going to take what satisfies me. But I'm really trying to have both." They can't see they're destroying one to get the other.

Even when trying to make a correction, Samson quickly reverted to his demanding self. Although he showed up with a goat to make peace and resume a relationship, he said:

> *"I will go in to my wife in the chamber." But*
> *her father would not allow him to go in.*
> **JUDGES 15:1**

Here's the problem. At the end of the betrothal—when the husband and the wife were supposed to consummate the marriage—Samson was away killing 30 people to meet his clothing obligation. So the father gave his daughter to the best man. And when the strongest guy in the universe showed up again, he didn't like the bad news. Sensual wanderers don't like bad news, especially "You can't have what you want" news. Judges 15:2 describes the father's hasty explanation:

> *Her father said, "I really thought that you utterly hated her,*
> *so I gave her to your companion. Is not her younger sister*
> *more beautiful than she? Please take her instead."*
> **JUDGES 15:2**

We can read between the lines: "Don't hurt me, please!" He feared for his life. Samson said:

> *This time I shall be innocent in regard to the Philistines,*
> *when I do them harm.*
> **JUDGES 15:3**

Samson went crazy, blaming everyone else beforehand for what he was about to do. Why was he so angry when the pretty sister was offered to him? Because he wasn't rational; he was sensual. His wasn't a thoughtful or logical response; it was a sensual response. It was a feeling reaction: "I want what I want. Get out of my way!" That's the life of a sensual wanderer: "What I desire is my idol. It's in my heart, and I *have* to have it." That kind of thinking rejects reason. And the worst part of it was his blindness to his destructive, wandering pattern.

Has a desire ever blinded you to the way you were hurting others? What happened?

In a rage Samson used foxes dragging torches as weapons of mass destruction. This caused the death of his wife and in-laws. Then he killed a thousand Philistines, which brought him to a point of physical exhaustion. Completely spent, he finally turned to God, only to demand:

> *You have granted this great salvation by the hand of your servant,*
> *and shall I now die of thirst and fall into the hands of the*
> *uncircumcised?*
> **JUDGES 15:18**

God graciously opened a rock, and water flowed to meet Samson's need. But it didn't curb his sensual pursuit. He couldn't see the carnage he was leaving in his wake.

SENSUAL WANDERERS ARE GROWING WEAKER

The story of a sensual wanderer doesn't plateau or retrace its steps back home. If you're wandering from God into some form of sensuality, it's worse now than it was two months ago. It's feeding on itself. You may think, *I'm managing my sin*. No, it's managing you. And it's getting worse.

We rejoin Samson in Judges 16:

> *Samson went to Gaza, and there he saw a prostitute,*
> *and he went in to her.*
> **JUDGES 16:1**

Samson saw a prostitute and decided on the spot to have her. Two chapters ago he got his parents and his wife's parents involved. Not now. Not to the increasingly sensual wanderer. He saw, he wanted, he went, he took, he felt, and he got. It was his new normal. Samson went into the prostitute's house.

People were watching Samson, and they thought his decision presented an opportunity to destroy him:

> *The Gazites were told, "Samson has come here." And they*
> *surrounded the place and set an ambush for him all night at the*
> *gate of the city. They kept quiet all night, saying, "Let us wait till*
> *the light of the morning; then we will kill him." But Samson lay till*
> *midnight, and at midnight he arose and took hold of the doors of*
> *the gate of the city and the two posts, and pulled them up, bar and*
> *all, and put them on his shoulders and carried them to the top of*
> *the hill that is in front of Hebron.*
> **JUDGES 16:2-3**

Samson, what are you doing? "Well, I saw these gates, and I thought I could probably lift them. Nobody *else* can pick them up, but *I* can. I'm the strongest man. So I carried them up the hill and left them there."

Samson was a silly clown. His gifts and abilities were for God. He was supposed to use his strength to drive out the Philistines, but he was using it to entertain them. All he ever thought about was what pleased him.

Notice how the progression unfolds here. Living for pleasure pulls you in as it becomes increasingly dissatisfying. It takes more calories to get a sugar high. More alcohol must be consumed to get in a stupor. A bigger quantity of drugs is needed to produce a high. Greater exposure to pornography or something more perverse is required to get a sexual high.

Is a sensual wanderer you know getting worse and growing weaker?

If you know someone like that, ask God to show you what you can do to bring this wanderer home.

Sensual wanderers get worse and grow weaker. Sensual wanderers think, *I'll get close to the edge of the cliff, and then I'll stop. I won't go over.* But that's not what happens. When they get close to the edge, they hit the gas pedal. They give up all pretense of desiring right and good. Instead of stopping, they accelerate toward their own destruction.

Is that you? If you still care, stop while you can. Because the final destination, as we'll see tomorrow, isn't a good place to land.

IT'S NOT TOO LATE

We're looking at the sensual wanderer this week, and it's not a pretty sight when someone wastes God's gifts to pursue sensual desires. That's what we learn from the life of Samson. But God has more to show us as the beleaguered wanderer nears the end of his journey.

WHERE SENSUAL WANDERING LEADS

In Judges 16:4 the plot in Samson's life significantly thickened: **"After this he loved a woman in the Valley of Sorek."** She may have been an Israelite; this was a border region that changed hands almost yearly between the Philistines and Israel. Her name was Delilah. The lords of the Philistines went to her and said:

> *Seduce him, and see where his great strength lies, and by what means we may overpower him, that we may bind him to humble him. And we will each give you 1,100 pieces of silver.*
> **JUDGES 16:5**

It would appear that Delilah was an Israelite, because if she was a Philistine, they wouldn't have had to pay her. They would've told her this was a case of national security. Delilah said to Samson:

> *Please tell me where your great strength lies, and how you might be bound, that one could subdue you.*
> **JUDGES 16:6**

What follows among Samson, Delilah, and the Philistines is a deadly cat-and-mouse game. Judges 16:5-22 records three rounds of the dangerous game: "I'll give you what you want if you tell me what I want." It turns into a wicked contest among sensual people.

Read Judges 16:5-22. What stands out to you about Delilah?

What stands out to you about Samson?

For all his physical strength, Samson was a moral and sensual weakling, participating in his own destruction. What was wrong with Samson? Are we to believe he didn't realize he was being played? Evidently not:

> *When she pressed him hard with her words day after day,*
> *and urged him, his soul was vexed to death.*
> **JUDGES 16:16**

Vexed means *bothered* or *annoyed*. It literally means *it was cut short*. He just didn't have the strength to keep the game going:

> *He told her all his heart, and said to her, "A razor has never come*
> *upon my head, for I have been a Nazirite to God from my mother's*
> *womb. If my head is shaved, then my strength will leave me, and*
> *I shall become weak and be like any other man."*
> **JUDGES 16:17**

Samson gave Delilah everything she wanted so that he could get everything he wanted. She immediately realized she'd broken through his last defenses. When her betrayal was accomplished, **"she began to torment him" (v. 19)**. Delilah *enjoyed* winning this deadly game. Her own sensual lusts needed to be satisfied, and defeating Samson must have been thrilling for her. When the Philistines rushed in, bound him, and gouged out his eyes, Delilah wasn't crying, "Stop! I love him! Don't hurt him!" She'd been tormenting him to wake him up. *To torment* means *to profane*. She was mocking him: "In your face now, strong boy!" She was hateful toward him. And he was so naïve, so blinded by his sensual focus, that he never saw the betrayal until his eyes were destroyed. Now he was a pathetic shell of a man.

What signs of self-destruction have you seen in a sensual wanderer?

SENSUAL WANDERERS WILL BE ABANDONED BY GOD

God has certain responses to our sensual wandering. God the Father sometimes lets us continue in our sensual behavior to learn the futility of life without Him. He abandons us to the consequences of our choices in hopes that we'll return to Him.

Describe a time when God let you experience consequences of a bad choice.

How sad that Samson, who was raised to live a life in God and for God, lived so far apart and yet so precariously close to the one thing he truly needed:

He awoke from his sleep and said: I will go out as at other times and shake myself free.
JUDGES 16:20

When you're falling into sensual pleasure, you think, *I can shake myself free at any point. I'm not going to get caught in this sin.* And for a time it appears you can succeed. Eventually, however, the sensual quest takes control, and you can't get away. Sin desires to have you. Sin desires to rule over you. For a time Samson could shake himself free and do something for God. But eventually, he came to the place where God gave him over to his pursuit. Suddenly God's grace was no longer stirring in his heart. And he couldn't shake himself free.

One of the saddest phrases in the Old Testament is at the end of Judges 16:20: **"He did not know that the LORD had left him."** Samson had lived outside God's will so long that he didn't sense the vacuum of His absence. He didn't know the Lord had removed His power from his life.

You might say, "Are you trying to scare me?" Yes, I am. If there's still time for you to be scared, I want you to be terrified. You can't tiptoe out of a sensual life; it takes the radical turnaround the Bible calls repentance. Jesus said:

If your right eye causes you to sin, tear it out and throw it away. For it is better that you lose one of your members than that your whole body be thrown into hell. And if your right hand causes you to sin, cut it off and throw it away. For it is better that you lose one of your members than that your whole body go into hell.
MATTHEW 5:29-30

What's your reaction to these verses? Is there a sensual sin in your life that's dragging you away from God?

God will eventually abandon the sensual wanderer. If you ask whether there's still time for you, I can say, based on the grace of Christ, "Yes, if you care." But repentance will cut you all the way to the bone. You'll have to let go of everything from your old life that isn't of God.

Samson lost everything before he realized he could have the one thing that really mattered. Was it over for him? It looked like it. It may seem that way in your life right now. But if you're still reading this, there's hope. It wasn't too late for Samson, and it isn't too late for you. When Samson's life had been reduced to a grind in the dark, things may have seemed hopeless for a while, **"but the hair of his head began to grow again" (Judg. 16:22).** The symbol of his heart for God began to return.

> **When you've been far from God, what signs did God give you that it wasn't too late to return to Him?**

> **What hope can you see for a sensual wanderer you're acquainted with?**

IT'S NOT TOO LATE FOR SENSUAL WANDERERS TO COME HOME

The clock might be winding down, but it's not too late. With all your sin, all your shame, all your defeat, and all your addictions, it's not too late.

Not being able to see may have been the greatest mercy to Samson as a sensual wanderer. As he trudged around and around grinding in that mill, no longer could he see things that lured him into sin. Maybe being in that prison was the best thing that happened to him because his feet couldn't wander toward sensuality. God, in His mercy, had put Samson on lockdown. Samson had a lot of time to think about who he was and what he had become.

Because of their shared history, the Philistines hated Samson. His story ends when he was brought to a big party so that the Philistines could mock him and make sport of him. His hair had grown back, but of course he still couldn't see. They led him up before the crowd so that they could ridicule him.

As the Philistines jeered, Samson said to the servant leading him, **"Let me feel the pillars"** **(v. 26).** With three thousand people on the roof (see v. 27), Samson prayed:

> *O Lord GoD, please remember me and please strengthen me only this once, O God, that I may be avenged on the Philistines for my two eyes.*
> **JUDGES 16:28**

His final request strikes us as sad. How about being avenged for disgracing God? Or for destroying your life? How about being avenged for denying your mission? But for his eyes? Yet God in grace answered his request and enabled him to kill the Philistines in attendance. So in spite of himself, Samson fulfilled the purpose God had planned for him in Judges 13:5.

Was Samson repentant? I don't know. But here's a note that blows me away: the Book of Hebrews lists Samson as a man of faith (see 11:32). In one dying act of faith, Samson called out to God and let Him use him for His purpose.

It wasn't too late for Samson, and it's not too late for the sensual wanderer. You don't have to say, "This is the way I am. I'm never going to be different." You *can* be different—not by your own power but by God's power released in you if you'll surrender to Him.

Read John 8:1-11. What does Jesus' response to the woman caught in adultery say to people who've wandered into sensual sin?

If you need to repent of sensual sin today, spend time in prayer. God loves you and wants you to be free. Ask Him to take the sin and shame and to forgive you.

If you know sensual wanderers, pray for an opportunity to tell them it's not too late to come home.

DAY 5

BRINGING THE WANDERER HOME

Sensual wanderers follow their own hearts no matter what. They live for themselves and, as a result, can be difficult to reach when we try to go get them and bring them back to God. Sensual wanderers are preoccupied with the gratification of their bodies. They're consumed with indulging their own desires. This tendency doesn't always manifest itself in sexual promiscuity. Sensual wanderers can be consumed with food, entertainment, legal substances, and illegal substances, as well as sexual sin.

> **Who immediately came to mind when you read the previous description? Refer back to the list you made in week 1. Take a moment and pray for the sensual wanderers on your list before continuing.**

FIND ENCOURAGEMENT IN THE FACE OF DISRESPECT

One trademark of sensual wanderers is that they're disrespectful. They don't respect God, the law, their calling, others, or themselves. It can be difficult to love a selfish person. It's likely the sensual wanderer will be disrespectful as you attempt to go bring them home.

> **Read Matthew 10:16-22. What do these verses say about being disrespected for speaking the truth?**

> **How can these verses encourage you in the face of disrespect from a sensual wanderer?**

SHARE LOVE AND TRUTH WITH THE SENSUAL WANDERER

Controlled by their appetites, sensual wanderers are oblivious to the carnage they're creating. They aren't rational or thoughtful. They may be unaware of the havoc they're producing by putting their desires over everything else.

How can you encourage a sensual wanderer to see the emptiness of his or her life?

It's important to recognize at this point that the pursuit of pleasure isn't the core problem for a sensual wanderer. God doesn't want us to live a cheerless existence devoid of pleasure. He has a blessed life in mind for us. Jesus assures us, "I came that they may have life and have it abundantly" (John 10:10). The core sin is placing sensual pursuits instead of God at the center of life.

How can you help a sensual wanderer realize the superior pleasure and abundance found in following Jesus?

How can you continue to demonstrate love for sensual wanderers who persist in their sin?

INVITE REPENTANCE AND OFFER FORGIVENESS

Sensual wanderers will get worse and worse before coming back home. If they stay on the path of self-gratification, God will eventually abandon them to the consequences of their choices. When you go after sensual wanderers, plan to help them see the need for repentance and forgiveness.

How would you explain repentance to someone who doesn't fully understand the concept?

Read Luke 17:3-4 and 2 Corinthians 7:8-12. What do these verses teach about confronting the sin of a sensual wanderer?

What encouragement do these verses give to go and get sensual wanderers?

TELL THE WANDERER IT'S NOT TOO LATE

Sensual wanderers may think it's too late to come home. They've wandered too far and done too much. The truth is that no one's gone too far. When we go and get sensual wanderers, we must emphasize that it's never too late. God used Samson, and He can use the sensual wanderers we know.

Read 1 John 1:9. What hope does this verse provide for a sensual wanderer?

How can we show a sensual wanderer that it's not too late?

Was there a time in your life when you thought it was too late, but God thought otherwise? How can you share that story with a sensual wanderer this week?

PRAY FOR THE SENSUAL WANDERER

Pray that God will open the eyes of the sensual wanderers you've identified in your life. Pray that He will help them recognize the havoc caused by their actions. Pray that the heart of the sensual wanderer will be open to repentance and returning to God. Pray for your own heart as you go get sensual wanderers. Pray that God will give you grace and forgiveness. Pray that you can encourage them to receive God's love and truth.

WILLFUL WANDERER, COME HOME

START

WELCOME BACK TO THIS GROUP
DISCUSSION OF *COME HOME.*

The previous session's application activity suggested making notes of ways our culture promotes sensuality. If you're comfortable, share your findings with the group.

Describe what you liked best about the lessons in week 4.
What questions do you have?

What does God offer that's missing in the life of a sensual wanderer?

Today's study will focus on the willful wanderer, or the prodigal. What comes to mind when you hear the word *prodigal?*

To prepare for the DVD segment, read aloud the following verses.

> *There was a man who had two sons. And the younger of them said to his father, "Father, give me the share of property that is coming to me." And he divided his property between them. Not many days later, the younger son gathered all he had and took a journey into a far country, and there he squandered his property in reckless living.*
> **LUKE 15:11-13**

WATCH

The willful wanderer is all about _____.

WHY A WILLFUL WANDERER LEAVES

1. _____ threatens control.

2. _____ threatens control.

3. _____ threatens control.

Freedom is an _____ in the heart of the willful wanderer.

WHEN A WILLFUL WANDERER COMES HOME

1. Pockets must be _____.

God is ordering all the circumstances, in His time, to bring the willful wanderer to the _____ of themselves.

2. The party must be _____.

The stronger the _____, the further the wanderer must go to get to the end.

3. Poverty must be _____.

The willful wanderer is the fool who never fears until they _____, the rebel who never rests until they hit rock bottom.

HOW A WILLFUL WANDERER REPENTS

1. The _____ awakens to reality.

To repent, they have to be without means and without _____.

2. The _____ submits to reality.

3. The emotions _____ to reality.

He's going to get everything he doesn't deserve, and he's not going to get what he does deserve. It's called _____ and _____.

WHAT A WILLFUL WANDERER FINDS WHEN HE COMES HOME

A healing _____, total _____, a _____ of his return, a _____ filled with hope

DISCUSS THE DVD SEGMENT WITH YOUR GROUP, USING THE QUESTIONS BELOW.

What's something new you learned from James's teaching about the prodigal son, the willful wanderer?

How has a desire for control caused you to rebel against God in the past?

What are some other reasons a willful wanderer walks away from God?

Respond to James's statement "The willful wanderer is the fool who never fears until they fall, the rebel who never rests until they hit rock bottom."

Why is it necessary for circumstances to explode before a willful wanderer comes home?

What signs of desperation have you seen in our culture that are results of willfully wandering from God?

How would you pray for a willful wanderer?

How did the father show grace and mercy to the prodigal son? How can you show God's grace and mercy to the wanderers you know?

Application. This week look for an opportunity to talk with a willful wanderer as a way of beginning a dialogue. Try to get an idea of what hope this person needs and how you can pray for his or her repentance and homecoming.

This week's Scripture memory.

I am sure that neither death nor life, nor angels nor rulers,
nor things present nor things to come, nor powers, nor height
nor depth, nor anything else in all creation, will be able to
separate us from the love of God in Christ Jesus our Lord.
ROMANS 8:38-39

Assignment. Read week 5 and complete the activities to conclude this study. Consider going deeper into this content by reading chapter 5 in James MacDonald's book *Come Home* (Moody Publishers, 2013).

WILLFUL WANDERER, COME HOME

We're beginning our final week of study together, and the wanderer we'll meet this week is the hardest one to deal with. It's the willful wanderer, someone who's deliberately chosen to walk away from God and, many times, from the families who love them as well. The Bible calls this wanderer a prodigal.

Prodigals can break your heart. I know because my daughter wandered from God for a time. Today she looks back and describes her hurt and stubbornness; her fear and loneliness; but most of all, her confusion. She lost sight of what home is, why it matters, and how to get back. How can wanderers come back home when they've lost all sense of direction? It takes a miracle of grace.

As a pastor, I think about the way the words in this week's study will be read and felt by those whose hearts are heavy for prodigals. We often feel helpless when we're waiting for wanderers to come home. I know how helpless Kathy and I felt when our daughter was wandering. But she came home, and your willful wanderer can too. Don't ever stop believing that God's love can bring your wanderer home.

If you know a willful wanderer, you're aware of people, situations, and needs that are waiting on God's timing. Will you trust God while you wait on Him to bring your wanderer home?

WHY DOES A WILLFUL WANDERER WANDER?

In this study we've looked at the fearful wanderer, the doubtful wanderer, and the sensual wanderer, and we've examined a biblical character who exemplifies each type. Our study's been driven by the imperative James delivered for all of us to find the wanderers and bring them home:

> *My brothers, if anyone among you wanders from the truth and someone brings him back, let him know that whoever brings back a sinner from his wandering will save his soul from death and will cover a multitude of sins.*
> **JAMES 5:19-20**

This week we come to the willful wanderer, someone who intentionally turns his back on God and His truth.

Do you know a willful wanderer? What words would you use to describe that person?

Of course, the most famous wanderer in Scripture is the prodigal son, whom Jesus introduced in Luke 15. Let's take a fresh look at this familiar parable to make sure we understand what's going on in the willful wanderer's mind and how we can bring the prodigal back to God. Jesus began:

> *There was a man who had two sons. And the younger of them said to his father, "Father, give me the share of property that is coming to me." And he divided his property between them. Not many days later, the younger son gathered all he had and took a journey into a far country, and there he squandered his property in reckless living.*
> **LUKE 15:11–13**

What reasons might have motivated the prodigal son to leave home?

What set these events in motion is a matter of the will. The son felt and exercised his power to decide. You'll never understand a willful wanderer intellectually because his decisions don't make sense. His choices don't add up. You can't get your mind around his thought process. Willful wandering isn't an intellectual thing. It's a matter of the will on autopilot: "It's my life. It's my vehicle. I'm driving. And that's the way it's going to be."

At the root of willful wanderers is this word: *control*. They're all about control. They may be headed over a cliff, but they're in control; that's all that matters. Anything that threatens control is a problem for the willful wanderer. We can see that principle in the life of the prodigal son.

Why does a willful wanderer leave? Here are three sample control issues.

AUTHORITY THREATENS CONTROL

Any authority threatens someone who feels he has to be in control. Jesus included the detail that the departing son was **"the younger" (v. 12)**. Was he spoiled? Was he too protected? Was he the only planet in his universe? We know that what he should have seen as a blessing, he saw as a burden. What he should have seen as provision and protection—like his family and his father's authority—he saw as a problem. This is always the way with a willful wanderer. Any source of authority threatens control.

How did you react to authority when you were a teenager?

What expressions of authority make you want to rebel as an adult?

The way Jesus unfolded the story at the end of verse 12 is interesting. When the younger son asked for his share of the property, the father surprisingly went along with the plan. Does that make sense to you? I'm thinking, *Hello, Dad! How about no?*

Refusal seems so obvious until you've faced off with someone determined to clash over wills. What you begin to learn with a willful opponent is that any assertion of authority makes conditions worse; resistance simply pushes them further away.

Negotiating also doesn't work with someone bent on control. You might be thinking, *Why couldn't the father just give the son a part of the farm and build a dividing fence?* Your plan would make sense if the son hadn't had huge control issues.

The Pharisees are good examples of people with huge control issues. These Jewish religious leaders claimed to have favor with God because they rigorously kept the law. In reality, however, they were hypocrites who knew nothing about a genuine relationship with God.

> **Read Matthew 21:23-27. Why did the Pharisees want to know by what authority Jesus healed and taught?**

When the Son of God came on the scene, He threw the Pharisees' entire world off balance because He threatened their control of the religious system. They had to maintain control even if it meant going against the authority of God Himself.

PROXIMITY THREATENS CONTROL

The last thing willful wanderers want is the beady eyes of authority looking at them all the time. They can't bear the possibility. In Jesus' story, even though the son had the money, he needed to leave. He had to put some space between him and anyone who'd threaten his control. Jesus described the departure:

> *Not many days later, the younger son gathered all he had and took a journey into a far country.*
> **LUKE 15:13**

If you've ever been in that father's position, it's very painful watching the willful wanderer pull out the suitcase and pack up the things. You want to yell, "Stop! Think! There's no future in this." But he's not thinking about the future. He's thinking only about himself and the present.

The young man went to **"a far country."** He had to get away from the person with the rules. He had to create distance from the place with control-threatening authority.

POLICY THREATENS CONTROL

A willful wanderer has his own declaration of independence: "I reject any system or any rules designed to dictate to me that I can't operate on the basis of my whims." Notice how quickly Jesus summarized the course of events:

> *[He] took a journey into a far country, and there*
> *he squandered his property in reckless living.*
> **LUKE 15:13**

The son wasted a sizable stake. Literally, the language means he scattered it. He pulled into town and announced, "Hey, everybody! The drinks are on me! Get me a room. Get me a woman. I don't care how much it costs." His pockets were bursting with wealth, and he foolishly squandered it. He couldn't imagine his funds as a diminishing resource. He saw them only as something to spend lavishly.

Such a person is so excited to have the apparent freedom to do whatever he wants to do that he can't see disaster rushing toward him. Freedom is an idol in the heart of a willful wanderer. Authority, proximity, and policy threaten his absolute need for control.

Identify a time when you rebelled against control. What influences were you trying to escape from?

What did you learn from that experience?

Why do willful wanderers hate rules so much? There are basically three reasons.

A LACK OF FAITH. Willful wanderers don't believe God's rules are good for their protection. They don't trust His character, and they resent His intrusion.

Read Matthew 19:16-22. How was the rich young man who met Jesus trying to hold on to control?

What did he miss by following his own way?

A LACK OF HUMILITY. Willful wanderers too prideful or stubborn to admit when they're wrong. You might suggest, "A few people have done what you're doing. It didn't work out too well for them. Would you like to hear their stories?"

"No! Absolutely not!" is their answer.

A LACK OF SELF-CONTROL. At the end of the day, the reasonableness of the rules isn't important to a person who's driven by autonomous desire. The willful wanderer has a condition called *wanderlust,* an old German word. Wanderlust is the desire to be on the road, to be moving, to be somewhere new, to leave all restraints behind. Many people can look to a time in their lives when they made bad decisions prompted by wanderlust.

At this point the far country has placed a merciful distance between the prodigal and his loved ones. His implosion is too painful to watch. Here's a warning to the parents of a prodigal: don't try to bind him or her too close during this difficult time, even as you pray it will end, or the proximity may destroy any possibility of a future return. Maintaining control is such a big deal to the willful wanderer that he often overreacts irrationally to any efforts to hold him down.

Do you know willful wanderers? What control are they rebelling against?

What have been the results of their wandering?

Because of the willful wanderer's desire for control, you may not be able to make contact with him if he's left home and gone to a far country, either physically, emotionally, or spiritually. But he's not beyond the reach of your prayers. Start regularly praying that any willful wanderers you know will come to a sense of futility and long for God and home.

DAY 2

WHEN DOES A WILLFUL WANDERER COME HOME?

We're studying the willful wanderer this week. As a pastor, I hear this question far too often: When will my willful wanderer come home? Hopefully, the willful wanderer will figure it out, the call will come, the soft knock will echo down the hallway. God uses circumstances to break the will of the wanderer. Not arguments. Not proof of the foolishness or the danger. Not tearful appeals or guilt trips. Not power plays, forced conformity, or common sense.

Here's when the willful wanderer comes home: the hammer has to fall. That's the way it really is. The crushing and merciless weight of reality is the most effective means to bring a willful wanderer home. So don't get between the hammer and the work. God's got to do it. God has to bring the person to his knees. Make sure you're not nourishing or supporting an artificial sense of well-being when the willful wanderer really needs the train to come off the rails.

What changes in circumstances might cause a wanderer to come home?

Let's look at some of the circumstances God uses to bring a willful wanderer home, based on Jesus' parable of the prodigal son in Luke 15.

POCKETS MUST BE EMPTY

When the money runs out, reality starts setting in. That's the first hint of trouble. Notice verse 14: **"When he had spent everything …"** The prodigal son had nothing left. I take the Bible literally, so when Jesus said *everything,* I don't think the boy was down to a few bucks. He was flat broke.

Family life in those days was tied to property ownership. To get his inheritance early— a third of the entire estate—the younger son had torn his family apart. But now his formerly full pockets were empty. In the past he would've turned to his family to bail him out. Now the wanderer needed what he had previously rejected. He needed what he had left in the dust.

Are you a willful wanderer? Do you find yourself at the place where your formerly full pockets are empty? You thought you had so much and it would last so long. Where has that plan left you? It's not what you thought, is it? It's not as good. It's not as fun. It's not as free. Satan promises freedom and gives bondage, slavery, addiction, devastation, and disease. He's a liar! And the only thing worse than falling for his lies is falling for them for a lifetime. Realizing the lies is a call to the willful wanderer to come home.

If you've ever intentionally wandered from the Lord, describe the emptiness that came with the realization that what you pursued didn't satisfy.

THE PARTY MUST BE ENDED

If we could intervene in this boy's life between verses 14 and 15, we'd probably say, "Dude! Come home right now!" But he was still fighting for control. Jesus continued, **"He went and hired himself out" (v. 15)**. This kid probably hadn't worked a day in his life. He was about to discover the reality of no skills in the marketplace.

The son who ran away was probably between 18 and 20 years old; otherwise, he wouldn't have been eligible to receive his father's inheritance. He certainly wouldn't have been able to travel to a different country. He was a foreigner in a **"far country" (v. 13)**. His age, background, and lack of experience added up to one conclusion: he wasn't very hirable. Notice the job he got:

> *He went and hired himself out to one of the citizens of*
> *that country, who sent him into his fields to feed pigs.*
> **LUKE 15:15**

It's almost impossible for us living in North America to comprehend what went off in the minds of a Jewish audience when they heard that this Jewish young man was feeding pigs. The Jewish people were forbidden to eat pork. Actually, the rabbis taught that anyone who bred swine was cursed. When Jesus got to this point in the story, there must have been a significant reaction from the audience. This boy was doing the unthinkable.

If you've wandered from God before, identify any signs of desperation you resorted to in order to maintain your lifestyle.

Identify any desperation you've observed in the life of a willful wanderer.

Picture the younger son struggling under a type of yoke over his shoulders that supported two heavy pails of slop. And he's walking among the pigs, scooping feed that only a pig would look at. The party was now officially over.

Was he broken? Close. Was he coming home? Not yet. The stronger the will, the further the wanderer must go to get to the end.

If you know a willful wanderer, identify the circumstances that need to change for that person to wake up and come home.

POVERTY MUST BE EXPERIENCED

The prodigal son was about to experience poverty as almost no one growing up in a North American context has ever experienced. Even people living on welfare in our society are nowhere close to poverty by a world standard. Prodigals have to discover firsthand the reality of authentic poverty. They have to experience it.

The young man was reaching his breaking point. His boss:

> ... *sent him into his fields to feed pigs. And he was longing to be fed with the pods that the pigs ate.*
> **LUKE 15:16**

He was so hungry that he was willing to put his face in filth to satisfy his hunger. Now that's poverty up close and personal. The willful wanderer never saw this coming. He was so protected and so well provided for in his sheltered upbringing that it never really occurred to him, nor did he have any basis for understanding, what was really out there in the world.

So off he went to join the stream of willful wanderers throughout history. Like the one who walked away from his marriage and his family. Or the one who left her parents and siblings behind to exercise control and experience freedom—the great idol—but ultimately experienced humiliation and shame at the end of the road. When the prodigal son chose to sin, he chose to suffer.

Here comes the reality of poverty. The willful wanderer is a fool who never fears until he falls. The willful wanderer is a rebel who never rests until he hits rock bottom. The willful wanderer isn't coming home until she's carrying a framed diploma from the School of Hard Knocks. The indelible experience is what she brings with her: "I get it now! I get it!" She's not coming back until she does.

Poverty must be experienced. Jesus' description of the moment includes this insight: **"He was longing" (v. 16).** The young man longed for what should have been loathsome to him. He badly wanted what was waste to others. That's a picture of poverty. His desperation broke his will.

Listen, willful wanderer. Are you ready yet? Are you ready yet to admit the escape hasn't given you what you thought it would give? Are you ready to say, "I've wandered far enough; I don't want this anymore. I can see where this is going, and I don't want to go there"? Are you ready to stop; turn back; humble your stubborn heart; and say to God, your family, and your church, "I want a change in my life; I want something different. It's not what I thought. I want what I had. I want to come home"?

Why is poverty necessary to bring a willful wanderer back to God?

Have you ever experienced that kind of poverty? Describe it.

You might ask, Can a willful wanderer really change? Yes, absolutely. I've heard the reports. I've seen the evidence. I can bear witness to people I know who can say, "I was a total prodigal. Against all odds God brought me home." Wanderers can return. God Himself is in the process of reaching them for that very purpose.

But they have to repent. They have be desperate enough to turn away from sin and turn toward God. They have to open their hearts to God in order to truly change. The prodigal is the poster boy for genuine repentance.

Ask God to identify any rebellious ways in your heart and in your life. Confess any ways you're wandering from God's will, repent, and return to your Father.

HOW DOES A WILLFUL WANDERER REPENT?

This week we're examining Jesus' story of the prodigal son in Luke 15 to identify the ways of the willful wanderer. I hope you're facing up to any rebellion in your own life, as well as discovering ways you can bring willful wanderers back to God.

Yesterday we said a prodigal has to repent in order to truly change and come home. Let's look at the steps involved in heartfelt repentance that brings life change.

THE MIND AWAKENS TO REALITY

When we last saw the prodigal, he was hip deep in a pig wallow, considering the menu before him:

> *He was longing to be fed with the pods that the pigs ate, and no one gave him anything. But when he came to himself ...*
> **LUKE 15:16-17**

That's the awakening moment, and it happens in a split second. The lightbulb goes on. The NASB translates that last phrase **"when he came to his senses."** The realization was sudden and painful: "What am I doing? Sin doesn't satisfy. Selfishness doesn't work." Two things have to come together for the mind to awaken to reality.

1. *Prodigals have to be without means.* As long as they still have means, prodigals will try something else stupid. They must run out of ways to get into further trouble.

2. *Prodigals have to be without inclination.* If they have inclination, prodigals are still on the road. They have to be unable to want control, autonomy, or the last word.

When the means is gone and the inclination has left, there's going to be a wake-up moment. There's going to be a snap back to reality.

Here's an important caution for those waiting for a prodigal to come home. Despite his sudden discovery of the obvious, we ought not to be harsh with the willful wanderer.

Prodigals can't see the truth. Rhetoric won't open their eyes. But when the party's over and the poverty's experienced, they're going to come to their senses. When their condition is desperate enough, their mind awakens to reality.

What realities were you blind to during a time of wandering or rebellion?

If you've wandered before, what awakening caused you to come back?

THE WILL SUBMITS TO REALITY

After awaking to reality, the young man in Jesus' parable began to assess his situation, rethinking where he came from. His reasoning was very practical:

> *How many of my father's hired servants have more than enough bread, but I perish here with hunger!*
> **LUKE 15:17**

Hired servants were day workers. They didn't belong to the household. During harvest the father would go to the marketplace and ask, "Does anybody want a job? We've got extra work." He'd hire them and pay them cash at the end of the day. Even those guys got enough from the boy's generous father. So the son drew some preliminary conclusions.

Now we see the wanderer's will engaging with the new reality:

> *I will arise and go to my father, and I will say to him, "Father, I have sinned against heaven and before you. I am no longer worthy to be called your son."*
> **LUKE 15:18-19**

When there's real repentance, there's also an awareness of how our sin affects God and others. The thing the prodigal couldn't see was now incredibly obvious. His mind awakened to reality, and his will submitted to it. He decided to go home, tell his father he was wrong, and cast himself on his father's mercy. His will submitted to reality and formed a plan of action.

That step is really important, because repentance is more than regret. It's not enough for us to simply feel bad for the mess we've created. Paul wrote:

I rejoice, not because you were grieved, but because you were grieved into repenting. For you felt a godly grief, so that you suffered no loss through us. For godly grief produces a repentance that leads to salvation without regret, whereas worldly grief produces death.
2 CORINTHIANS 7:9-10

What's the difference between godly grief and worldly grief?

How have you experienced godly grief after wandering from God?

Worldly repentance is regret. Sorry I got caught. Sorry I look bad. Sorry I feel bad. Sorry I've upset you. Worldly sorrow doesn't drive us from death but toward it. That's not repentance. The boy's words in Luke 15:18-19 show repentance. He came to his senses; that was his mind. **"I will arise and go" (v. 18);** that was his will submitting to reality.

EMOTIONS CONFORM TO REALITY

When he lived at home, the prodigal had taken all the great things about his life for granted. He'd demanded his inheritance without a hint of gratitude. Now reality had given him the news that he deserved nothing. He'd decided to return home, but he wasn't assuming that he could resume his place. He knew he must admit to his father, **"I am no longer worthy to be called your son" (v. 19).**

Was that true? It was absolutely true. He *wasn't* worthy. What he said and did forfeited his right to be treated as a son.

Considering that young man's situation, aren't you glad that in God's family we don't operate on rights? God doesn't treat us as we deserve to be treated. This kid deserved nothing, and he knew it. Yet that's why the kingdom of God is so awesome—because he was going to get everything he didn't deserve, and he wasn't going to get what he did deserve—just like us. It's called God's grace and mercy.

How did you experience grace and mercy when you came back to God after a season of wandering?

Once the prodigal's emotions conformed to reality, he made his way home:

> *He arose and came to his father. But while he was still a long way off, his father saw him and felt compassion, and ran and embraced him and kissed him. And the son said to him, "Father, I have sinned against heaven and before you. I am no longer worthy to be called your son."*
> **LUKE 15:20-21**

It went beyond a thought process; the boy actually did it—an indication of true repentance. And the father was waiting and watching. The wanderer hadn't even been thinking about home, but he'd been thought about, loved, prayed for, and released to God.

Did the father just happen to be looking in that direction when his son was coming down the road? Probably not. He was likely going every day and looking. Day after day he was scanning the horizon and longing for the return of the son he loved. All the hopes, all the dreams, all the plans, all the prayers—they were all for this day.

> **Think about a wanderer you know. List some things he's missing by not being in fellowship with his Father.**

The waiting father did more than see his son. He felt compassion (see v. 20). That word means *to feel for the other person*. Instead of any hint of rejection, punishment, conditions, or hesitance to receive the wanderer back, the father's heart reached for him long before his feet began to move. That's God's heart—instantly and overwhelmingly responsive to a repentant sinner. As authentic people of God, we always need to reflect His heart.

The son came as he was. Ashamed. Embarrassed. Foolish, not to mention filthy from working on the hog farm. And rehearsing his speech: "This is how it worked out, Dad. I was so sure, but I was so wrong. I was so determined, but I was so misguided." Trudging over the last hill, he was ready for the moment of truth.

The son came home.

> **If you've been a willing wanderer, are you ready to come home? Tell God what's on your heart today. Or maybe as you've read these pages, you've wept for loved ones or friends who need to come home. Spend time in prayer for them.**

DAY 4
COME HOME

The prodigal son wandered and suffered greatly in the process. But yesterday we saw his mind awake to reality, his will submit to reality, and his emotions conform to reality. Now it was time for him to come home. How would he be treated when he came back?

> If you've ever wandered away from God, what kind of reception did you find when you came back to Him?

GOD WELCOMES THE WANDERER HOME

Each wanderer has a question: What will I find when I come home? The prodigal's thoughts reveal one of the things any willful wanderer is concerned about: "If I admit who I really am—if I acknowledge what I've really done—what kind of reception will I get?" Jesus tells us God's answer to that question in His story.

A HEALING EMBRACE. The prodigal son didn't expect the sight of his father running toward him. In all Scripture we see God running only one time. He doesn't run to church. He doesn't run to the mission field. *But He runs to a repentant sinner.* That's what Jesus' story is all about.

The son tried to get the words out, but his father was all over him. Jesus said the father **"embraced him and kissed him" (Luke 15:20).** The phrase means *kissed him repeatedly.* He threw his arms around him and held on to him, no doubt weeping for joy.

The father in Jesus' story represents God the Father, so his action indicates the reception a willful wanderer will get from God Himself. When wanderers come back to God, they're welcomed with a hug like no other. The father overwhelmed the son with an embrace and kisses. Embraced by the arms of God the Father, wanderers come home to the sense that they're loved no matter where they've been or what they've done.

If we're going to take seriously the command to go get the wanderer, we'd better be prepared to follow God's lead in the reception we give to those who come home.

Read the following verses and describe God's love for those who come to Him.

Jeremiah 31:3

Romans 8:38-39

God loves you. He wants you to come home. Come home to a healing embrace.

TOTAL FORGIVENESS. It was finally time for the son's confession, so well rehearsed over the agonizing miles:

> *The son said to him, "Father, I have sinned against heaven and before you. I am no longer worthy to be called your son."*
> **LUKE 15:21**

The father, however, wouldn't enter that discussion. He didn't even answer the son because he'd already made his statement with his embrace and kisses.

The son was still trying to get through his speech when his dad began to issue orders:

> *The father said to his servants, "Bring quickly the best robe, and put it on him, and put a ring on his hand, and shoes on his feet."*
> **LUKE 15:22**

"Quick! Bless and refresh him. He's home; let's make him look the part! He doesn't owe me anything. I'm not looking to get. I want to give more now that he's ready to receive. I've been longing for this." The father's words epitomized total welcome and restoration. What a beautiful picture of forgiveness.

CELEBRATION. Verse 23 continues the father's commands: **"Bring the fattened calf."** A family with means would have always had on hand an animal raised for a festive occasion. The father had been planning for a special event: "Bring it and kill it and let's eat and celebrate. It's time!"

Don't ever wonder how God the Father feels when a wanderer comes home. All of Luke 15 describes the celebration that goes on in heaven for all the work and prayer behind the scenes to make possible the moment of humility and homecoming. You can bless the heart of God. You can kick off a true party in your honor, willful wanderer. Come home to a celebration of your return.

A FUTURE FILLED WITH HOPE. The father's words over his returned son ought to take our breath away: **"This my son was dead, and is alive again; he was lost, and is found" (v. 24).** Dad had thought it was over; his son wasn't coming back. He had almost lost hope. The departure of a willful wanderer feels like a death in the family, but his return is like a resurrection. The wanderer was alive and found. Now a future filled with hope is possible. What a welcome to come home to!

> **If you've been praying for a specific wanderer, write down some of the things he'd come home to if he returned to God.**

TO THE WANDERER

Much of this week's study has necessarily focused on comfort and understanding for the family of the willful wanderer. But its highest objective and purpose are for you, the wanderer. Maybe you've made choices you shouldn't have made, and they've taken you to places you didn't want to go. And if you can admit that, what would keep you from coming home, first to God your Father and then to those who love you?

Sin will always cost more than we want to pay. It will always bring us to poverty in ways we never imagined. Whatever your previous impression, the true church of Jesus Christ is filled with loving people who've been in the place where you are now.

Wanderer, maybe you've never given your life to Christ, never acknowledged Him as the Lord of your life. But today you want to come home to the God who loves you, who sent His Son to pay for your sin. Or maybe you've known the truth, but you've been living apart from it. And you need to turn and return. This is your opportunity to come home.

You're one courageous decision away from the most important turn in your life. You may not have another opportunity like this. So if God is stirring truth in your heart, have courage and make a change. The Bible says all of heaven rejoices, not over 99 people who don't see how poorly they're doing but over 1 person who truly repents (see v. 7). God the Father is ready to throw a party in your honor if you'll tell Him with your words and your life that you're ready to come home.

> **If you've wandered from God, are you ready to come home? Tell God what's on your heart. Repent and come home today.**

BRINGING THE WANDERER HOME

The willful wanderer in Luke 15 is the most well-known wanderer in the Bible. We need to keep in mind, though, that not all willful wanderers are young rich kids. There are prodigals of all different ages and statuses. Willful wanderers hate control. They wander because they don't want to be bossed around—by God or anyone else.

Look back in week 1, day 5 at your list of the wanderers in your life. Identify any who fit the description of a willful wanderer. Keep them in mind as you complete today's lesson.

WATCHING AND WAITING

The difficult thing about willful wanderers is that we must wait for God to bring them home. There are things we can do to help, but ultimately, God must orchestrate the circumstances that will break the will of these wanderers.

Do you know anyone who was once a willful wanderer? Perhaps you were at one time. What happened that brought them or you back home?

It's easy to resent a willful wanderer's return. The wanderer's been out having fun, being selfish, and ignoring instruction while you've been faithful. It can be difficult to find compassion for him. The father in the story did. The brother didn't.

Read Ephesians 4:32. How can you show compassion to wanderers who haven't yet returned?

How can you demonstrate compassion to wanderers who've returned?

Willful wanderers are difficult to bring home. They don't like control, and your going to get them may seem to them like an effort to control them. This is especially true if you're close to the wanderer. Taking steps to get willful wanderers will involve discomfort and risk because they won't like your efforts to bring them back. Going and getting them can be painful, and it will be uncomfortable. But the reward is worth it.

What's something you can do this week to help bring home the willful wanderers you know?

WELCOME BACK THE PRODIGAL

The father in Luke 15 shows us how we should welcome back willful wanderers. He embraced his son, forgave him, celebrated his return, and looked forward to the future.

What are some ways you can actively embrace returned wanderers?

How can you demonstrate forgiveness to a willful wanderer who's returned?

How will you celebrate the return of the wanderers in your life?

In what ways can you help a willful wanderer look forward to the future?

PRAY FOR THE WILLFUL WANDERER

Pray that God will bring the willful wanderer home in His time. Pray that the willful wanderer will come to the end of himself and turn back home when he finds himself at rock bottom. Pray that you'll be ready to receive the willful wanderer with compassion. Pray for wisdom in bringing the wanderer back home.

Also from
JAMES
MacDONALD

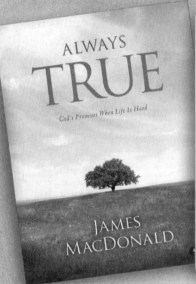

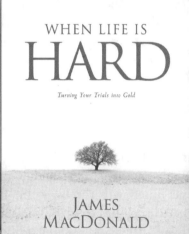

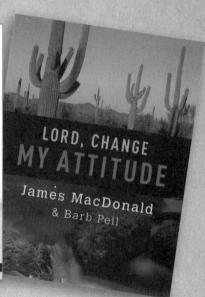

ALWAYS TRUE

Discover that God's promises are always true—that we can trust Him to be faithful to His Word no matter what we face. (6 sessions)

Member Book 005371573 **$11.95**
Leader Kit 005274675 **$99.95**

WHEN LIFE IS HARD

Learn how to deal with the trials of life, find hope through the process, and respond to them in a way that submits to God's work in your life and glorifies Him. (6 sessions)

Member Book 005293072 **$11.95**
Leader Kit 005271225 **$99.95**

LORD, CHANGE MY ATTITUDE

Lead others (and even yourself) out of attitudes that God hates and into those He honors. (11 sessions)

Member Book 005035039 **$14.95**
Leader Kit 005097385 **$149.95**

OTHER STUDIES BY
JAMES MACDONALD

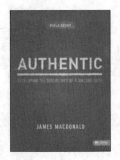

Authentic: Developing the Disciplines of a Sincere Faith

A lot of people call themselves Christians, but they've settled for lives of disobedience and half-hearted commitment to Christ. Authentic followers of Jesus, on the other hand, want to grow in His likeness, work for His kingdom, and do His will. This Bible study examines six spiritual disciplines that can help believers develop a more authentic relationship with Jesus: Bible study, prayer, fasting, fellowship, service, and worship. As our perfect example of authenticity, Jesus Himself practiced these disciplines and calls us to follow in His steps. Seven sessions.

Leader Kit 005399891 • Member Book 005470535

Vertical Church

Is your church experiencing a window-rattling, earth-shattering, life-altering encounter with the living God? James MacDonald rejects the idea that church has to be business as usual, preoccupied with a human-centered agenda. Only a vertical church can reveal a holy God who shows up in power, changing hearts and altering lives. This Bible study provides a biblical viewpoint on what it means for believers and churches to maintain a vertical focus on God and His kingdom. It describes our common longing for God, our common provision in God's presence, and our common access to God through Jesus. Then it identifies and teaches on four requirements for a church that is focused on God: unashamed adoration, unapologetic preaching, unafraid witness, and unceasing prayer. Eight sessions.

Leader Kit 005522646 • Member Book 005522647